THE DEEN BROS.

take it easy

THE DEEN BROS.

take it easy

quick and affordable meals the whole family will love

jamie and bobby deen

and melissa clark

BALLANTINE BOOKS · NEW YORK

Published in the United States by Ballantine Books, an imprint of
The Random House Publishing Group, a division of Random
House, Inc., New York.

BALLANTINE and colophon are registered trademarks of Random
House, Inc.

ISBN 978-0-345-51326-7

Printed in the United States of America on acid-free paper

People photographs and the photograph on pages xiv and 83
courtesy of Robert Jacobs Photography

www.ballantinebooks.com

9 8 7 6 5 4 3 2 1

First Edition

Book design by Liz Cosgrove

This book is dedicated
with love and respect
to our mom and dad.

SCHOOL DAYS 1951 '52
Verner

Paula Hiers, age nine, and Jimmy Deen, age seven.

Acknowledgments

To my wife, Brooke: Thank you for your support and your love that keeps my spirit in the clouds. To our beautiful son, Jack: Thank you for your big hugs, wet kisses, and for your "I love you, too, Daddy." I love you both down to the ground and up to the sky.

To Bobby, my best friend since I was three years old: Thanks for doing everything a little brother should do. . . . You made me a big brother.

A mighty and heartfelt thanks goes out: To all of our staff, guests, and friends at The Lady & Sons Restaurant and at Paula Deen Enterprises, who have helped shape, grow, and sustain our "little business that could." To Melissa Clark, who, while very pregnant, got it done. Again. To Barry Weiner and our literary agent, Janis Donnaud, for your hard work, gentle guidance, and the spot-on restaurant recommendations when we visit New York. To our editor, Pamela Cannon; publisher Libby McGuire; and the entire Ballantine team, thank y'all for helping make our dreams come true. To Robert Jacobs and Ben Fink for adding the art of their beautiful photography.

And, for their unlimited love and support, thanks goes out to: Uncle Bubba Hiers, Aunt Peggy Ort, Fred and Linda Terry, Michael Groover, Therlus Deen, Steven Farmer and all the folks at the University of Georgia, Gordon Elliot, Kate Neumann, Mary Jane Crouch, and our tireless assistant, Michael Peay.

— *Jamie Deen*

I'd like to thank the staff at The Lady & Sons. Without all of your hard work, this book wouldn't be possible. Thanks to my brother, Jamie, my business partner and friend. I admire and love you. Thank you, Mom and Dad, for teaching me what is really important in life. To my friend and coach Sam Carter, thank you for helping me be a better man. And to my friends Michael, Matt, Cindy, and Ashley, thank you for eating all of my cooking!

— *Bobby Deen*

Foreword by *Paula Deen*

Sometimes I just have to take a breath and marvel at the way time flies. It really does seem like yesterday that I had my two darling babies underfoot, peeking into the pots and pans bubbling away on the stove top, trying to figure out what I was fixing for dinner—and trying to steal themselves a taste. But here those two mischievous little boys have grown into two fine men, each with a heart as good as gold—and each just as interested as ever in what's in store for them at the dinner table. Well, I guess it's true that the apples don't fall far from the tree—you can sure believe that dinner is a favorite preoccupation of their mama's, too.

Mealtimes are still family time for us Deens, and it's gotten even more special now that Jamie and Brooke have brought our precious grandbaby, Jack, into the mix. That's what a baby can do to a family: take a heart that's already full up with love and make it even bigger to hold more love than you ever thought was possible. But having a baby did more than change our hearts; he changed the way we cook, too (though for the Deens, our hearts and our cooking are truly one and the same). Becoming a daddy has really turned Jamie's kitchen techniques around. When I pop in on them for dinner, I see Jamie and Brooke doing things on the quick, because they just can't afford to spend hours over the stove—and who would want to anyway? Especially when the weather's fine and they've got that little boy to take for a walk to the park (or, knowing my son, more likely to teach Jack how to throw a football).

And it's no different over at Bobby's house. Let me tell you a secret about my younger son: He is a marshmallow. He may not look like one, but that's exactly what he is. He's a sweet ol' softie when it comes to helping out a pal, whether that means extra practices with his softball team, a night out with his buddies, or setting up fund-raisers for charity (he even auctioned himself off as a date to benefit our local food bank). Because of his giving nature, his schedule is so jam-packed that he has had to teach himself how to make his meals on the double, without sacrificing one bit of that good old-fashioned Southern home-cooked taste he grew up on. You know, just because you have half the time does not mean you have half the appetite.

I couldn't be more gratified that in this book, Jamie and Bobby are sharing their quick and creative meals with busy families everywhere. I tell you, I wish I had had a cookbook like this back in the days when I had a young family to feed. Once again, I find myself amazed at what these two little boys (and no matter how much time passes, they will always be their mama's little boys) have accomplished.

And I know you and your family will enjoy every single delicious recipe my boys have to offer. Even if you've got time to kill (lucky you!), you'll still love the brilliant, easy dishes they've gathered for y'all right here. I just can't wait to dig in!

I love you boys!
xoxo, Mom

Contents

Introduction

We love food. It is our family's past, present, and future. Every bite of green bean takes us back to our Granny Paul's kitchen in Lee County, just outside Albany, Georgia, and her amazing garden. She would have us boys go out back and dig up the potatoes, snap the beans, cut the squash, wash the tomatoes, and pick the strawberries for her famous shortcake. She taught our mama, Paula Deen, to pass it on to us and others. Boy, did she ever!

For us, the end of a perfect day is when everybody's feet are under the same table. Mama always said the most special thing in the world is for the whole family to share a home-cooked meal. . . . Sure we have a couple of pizzas in the freezer, and there are always some cans of soup rolling around in the pantry for the nights when our schedules are too tight to cook. But we don't settle for that very often: Dinner is dinner, and we Deens don't mess with dinner.

As you may know, we are in the restaurant business. Our Savannah restaurant, The Lady & Sons, offers thirteen meals a week, employs more than 250 folks, and served more than a half million people in 2008. We also saw our first retail space, The Paula Deen Store, open, and that's a business we are still learning about every day. Plus, Jamie has a toddler at home, and Bobby is on his own, so most nights the fried chicken dinners with their slow-cooked collard greens, fresh creamed potatoes, and corn bread with cane syrup that were staples at Mama's table when we were kids are an improbability. We are just like y'all—too busy and still waiting on that eighth day of the week to pop up so we can get everything done. Between the restaurant, company softball team, travel for work, keeping up with our Georgia Bulldogs (Go, Dawgs!), friends to see, and yards to take care of, there is simply no time for the traditional big Southern feast on a Wednesday night. We do, however, still want to find the time to sit down and relax as a family. What better time than dinner around the table?

So how do we put home-cooked meals on the table, despite our overstuffed schedules? By using the business plan Mama taught us: Keep it simple. We stick to the recipes that are quick, easy, and tasty. These recipes can be prepared in forty-five minutes or less and won't break the bank, no matter how many hungry mouths you're feeding. And to make things even more convenient for y'all, while most of the recipes are designed to serve four, you can easily cut them in half, or double or triple them to serve a crowd.

Most nights, Jamie and Brooke meet up in the kitchen at 5 o'clock. All you parents know dinnertime is not set up on a slide rule—dinner is on the table at 6 o'clock. Jamie's son, Jack, makes sure of it! So we count on simple ingredients and fast favorites like **Speedy Mini Meat Loaves** (page 12) or the Deen family recipe for **Pimiento Mac and Cheese** (page 113) to get the job done. By the time Bobby gets home, he is way too hungry to start whisking up complicated sauces or prepping veggies. He is out the back door headed to the grill to get his **Easy After-Work BBQ Chicken** (page 91). Bobby's grill is the most-used piece of equipment at his house. It's his favorite way to create fast, good-for-you meals—and best of all, the kitchen stays clean.

Dinner at our homes has to be as easy to prepare as it is good to eat. If y'all have seen us on the Food Network on our show *Road Tasted* or read our first books, you know complicated cooking is not what we are about. The recipes in this book feature the food we eat at home, and our mama, the queen of slow cooking, loves the way we have tweaked the style and saved the essence. We have taken these flavors and updated them to keep up with our lives, so y'all will find them more streamlined than ever.

We keep it simple and affordable by using our favorite ingredients—rice, ground beef, canned tomatoes, cheese, and all the down-to-earth food that is easily found in every supermarket.

We still crave the deep rich flavors that Mama used to fix using basic ingredients and plenty of time back in the days when we were at school and she was home simmering soups and stews. Today, these meals mean throwing a handful of things into the crockpot before work and cooking up some noodles when we get home. Some of our modern favorites are done this way, so we have dedicated a whole chapter to getting those childhood flavors back on the table.

We are also trying to eat a *little* healthier . . . but let's be honest. We are Paula's boys, and we aren't going to set weight-loss records anytime soon. But we do try to enjoy our butter, heavy cream, and fried foods in moderation. We think some nights you have to swap a salad for a twice-baked potato or a grilled chicken breast for a bone-in rib-eye steak. We can satisfy a burger craving with our **Turkey and Black Bean Burgers with Corny Salsa** (page 44), and some nights a dinner-size salad like our **Spicy Honey Chicken Salad over Spinach** (page 150) really hits the spot. Sometimes we split the difference and balance both sides—a hearty dish like **Spicy Beef and New Orleans Red Rice Skillet Dinner** (page 5) with a lighter side dish, like **Aunt Peggy's Pickled Cucumber, Tomato, and Onion Salad** (page 6).

We have included some of our favorite side dishes with many of the entrées in this book. We think it's fun to mix and match the sides with different main dishes and find matches made in heaven. Y'all feel free to change it up and find your own family's favorite combinations. Just because Bobby loves to serve his **Broccoli and Red Bell Pepper Salad** (page 109) with his **Spicy Southern Shrimp and Pasta Bake** (page 108) doesn't mean you will . . . although it's a great marriage of flavors. The recipes here are flexible; when it comes time to put your meal together, go with your gut—and what's easiest. Stay relaxed in the kitchen, and it will help you relax at the table. It will make everything taste that much better.

And, of course, dessert; we never forget dessert. We can't tell you how many nights we have sat down to dig into pies and layer cakes and homemade meringues and cookies and fresh-churned ice cream. . . . Oh, we do love our mama. But at home for us now, we don't have the time to do any real baking. Instead, for those nights you deserve a little something extra, we'll show you how to use pantry staples to put together almost instant desserts. No matter how busy we are, we think there is always time for a sweet ending to a meal.

We know y'all are real busy and trying to watch your budget, but you're also looking for ways to keep home-cooked food on your table. It's about carrying on family traditions or, like with Jack, starting new ones. We hope y'all will enjoy how fast, simple, and economical these recipes are. If they can help you make time to enjoy a meal with loved ones, we've accomplished our goal.

—Bobby and Jamie

A Note on Well-Stocked Shelves

Our goal with this book is to give you ideas for meals that are quick and easy (not to mention satisfyingly scrumptious), so it kind of defeats the purpose if you have to run to the market every night to get together ingredients to make these dishes. It's best to maintain a stock of canned and dried goods with a long shelf life in the pantry, fresh ingredients that you'll use every day in the fridge, and just enough frozen food (if they're well wrapped, meat, fish, and poultry will keep for up to three months) to round out your recipe. Here's a list of the basic supplies we think you should keep on hand to make a complete Deen-style meal at the drop of a hat.

IN THE PANTRY
Long-grain rice
Dried pasta
Canned beans (kidney, pinto, chickpea, and baked)
Canned tomatoes
Prepared tomato sauce
Tabasco sauce
The Lady's House Seasoning (page 7)
White wine vinegar
Cream of mushroom soup
Cheddar cheese soup
Tortilla chips
Bisquick baking mix
All-purpose flour
Dark brown sugar
Chocolate chips
Marshmallow Fluff
Your favorite cookies

IN THE REFRIGERATOR
Unsalted butter
Milk
Heavy cream
Large eggs
Cream cheese
Sour cream
Bacon
Cheddar cheese
Parmesan cheese
Vidalia or yellow onions
Garlic
Cherry or grape tomatoes
Avocado
Bagged mixed greens
Romaine or Boston lettuce
Carrots
Celery
Lemons
Limes

Fresh ravioli or tortellini
Chicken broth
Salsa
Pesto sauce
Bottled ranch dressing
The Lady & Sons Honey Mustard Sauce (page 159)
Mustard
Ketchup
Whipped topping

IN THE FREEZER
Ground beef
Thick-cut pork chops
Boneless skinless chicken breasts and thighs
Hot or sweet sausage
Shrimp
Your favorite ice cream
Frozen whipped topping

SPICY BEEF AND NEW ORLEANS RED RICE SKILLET DINNER 5

Aunt Peggy's Pickled Cucumber, Tomato, and Onion Salad 6

MAMA'S HAMBURGER "HOBO SACKS" 7

The Lady's House Seasoning 7

EASY CHEESEBURGER CASSEROLE 8

Sliced Tomato and Onion Salad with Russian Dressing 9

JAMIE DEEN'S FIVE-LAYER BEEF TACO PIE 10

Taco Seasoning 11

SPEEDY MINI MEAT LOAVES 12

Roasted Sweet Potato Wedges with Brown Sugar and Cinnamon 14

BALSAMIC-GLAZED LONDON BROIL 15

Zesty Potato, Olive, and Pimiento Salad 17

BOBBY'S FAVORITE BEEF TERIYAKI STIR-FRY WITH BROCCOLI AND PEPPERS 18

Asian Greens and Radish Salad with Sesame Dressing 19

REAL EASY APPLE CIDER PORK TENDERLOIN 21

Garlic Mashed Potatoes 21

SMOTHERED PORK CHOPS AND RICE BAKE 22

ITALIAN-STYLE PORK CHOPS 23

DOUBLE ORANGE PORK CHOPS 24

Buttery Stone-Ground Grits 25

When we were growing up in Georgia, vegetarianism just wasn't on the menu. There was always plenty of meat in the house—especially ground beef, because it was affordable. And Mama found so many different things to do with ground chuck—from hamburgers to casseroles, from hobo dinners to taco pie and meat loaf—we never got sick of it. So it's no surprise that we're still big meat eaters.

We have, however, branched out a little. For one thing, we both love pork chops, which are quick to fix and satisfying to eat, whether you want to fry or grill them, smother them, or bake them with rice. Plus, we consider pork a little healthier than red meat. Either way, meat is featured at our dinner tables more nights than not.

The beauty of a good chop or roast is that you're practically done cooking by the time you've brought it home from the store. Add a hot pan or grill, a side or salad, and that's dinner. Plus, you can buy extra to cook enough for leftovers. Nothing's better than leftover steak or pork on a sandwich for lunch, or to turn into a main-course salad for supper the next day. Then you're ahead of the game, and we love it when we can get there without too much effort.

Whether we're trying something new with the ingredients we have on hand, like **Italian-Style Pork Chops** (page 23) made with marinara sauce and plenty of melted mozzarella, or making familiar family recipes like **Mama's Hamburger "Hobo Sacks"** (page 7), we just keep coming up with delicious ways to cook up meat for dinner. The recipes here are the dishes we crave when we're really hungry, and they are gratifying on so many levels. A hearty meal based around London broil or pork tenderloin can be as simple as you want, and it always makes everyone at the table feel satisfied and well taken care of.

Spicy Beef and New Orleans Red Rice Skillet Dinner

We always have a red rice dish on the buffet table at The Lady & Sons. Here we added beef to the skillet to turn our Cajun-influenced red rice dish into an easy crowd-pleaser. Since we're on the Georgia coast, we'll also do red rice with sausage and shrimp, so you can use that instead if you like: Just brown crumbled sausage in place of the beef and stir in a half pound of shelled shrimp for the last five minutes of simmering (or until they're pink).

SERVES 4

1 tablespoon olive oil

1 pound ground beef

2¼ teaspoons salt

2 celery ribs, diced, plus celery leaves, chopped, for garnish (optional)

1 medium onion, diced

½ green bell pepper, seeded and diced

2 cups chicken broth

One 14-ounce can tomato purée

1½ cups uncooked long-grain rice

1 teaspoon sugar

2 teaspoons Tabasco or other hot sauce

1. Heat the olive oil in a large skillet over high heat. Crumble the beef into the skillet and season with ½ teaspoon of the salt. Brown the beef, breaking it up with a fork, for 5 to 7 minutes, or until the meat is no longer pink. Transfer to a paper towel–lined plate to drain.

2. Reduce the heat to medium-high and pour off all but 2 tablespoons of the drippings from the skillet. Sauté the diced celery, onion, and bell pepper in the skillet for about 5 minutes, or until tender. Add the browned beef, chicken broth, 1½ cups of water, the tomato purée, rice, sugar, the remaining 1¾ teaspoons salt, and the Tabasco and bring to a boil.

3. Reduce the heat to medium-low and cook, covered, for 40 minutes, or until the rice is tender. Garnish with the chopped celery leaves (if desired).

Aunt Peggy's Pickled Cucumber, Tomato, and Onion Salad

Our Aunt Peggy doesn't serve a meal without this delicious salad. She sometimes makes a variation with banana peppers or bell peppers added in. It's such a simple, healthy side, and all you need to get dirty is your cutting board and one bowl. Its fresh garden flavor is a terrific complement to the spicy rice or just about any main course in the book, but we especially love it with Honey Mustard Baked Chicken (page 33) and any kind of pork chop (pages 22 to 24).

SERVES 4 TO 6

1 pound cucumbers (about 3 cucumbers), peeled and thinly sliced

1 pint cherry tomatoes, halved

½ Vidalia onion, very thinly sliced

2 tablespoons chopped fresh parsley

1 teaspoon apple cider vinegar

1 teaspoon olive oil

Salt and freshly ground black pepper to taste

In a bowl, toss together the cucumbers, cherry tomatoes, onion, parsley, vinegar, olive oil, salt, and pepper. Let the salad stand for 10 minutes before serving.

"Down South, we season with salt, pepper, and pork." — Jamie

Mama's Hamburger "Hobo Sacks"

As kids growing up, we always loved Mama's tasty "hobo" dinners. Super easy to make—she would just throw everything together in an aluminum foil packet—and easy on the wallet, these complete meals in a pouch were on the table each and every week. To dress up these humble-as-a-hobo meals for company, try adding baby carrots, fennel, and other root vegetables, along with some nice ground sirloin. The aluminum foil seals in all the flavor of the ingredients and makes the sacks—fancy or simple—even more delicious than they ought to be. And though they are a whole meal in themselves, we love to serve them with our Moist-and-Easy Corn Bread (page 45).

SERVES 4

1 pound ground beef

1 tablespoon The Lady's House Seasoning (recipe follows)

2 large carrots, peeled and sliced ⅛ inch thick

2 medium potatoes, peeled and sliced ⅛ inch thick

1 medium onion, cut into small chunks

4 tablespoons (½ stick) unsalted butter, cut into cubes

1. Preheat the oven to 400°F. Place four large sheets of aluminum foil (about 12 by 15 inches) on your work area.

2. Combine the beef with 2 teaspoons of the house seasoning and form into 4 equal-size patties. Place equal amounts of carrots, potatoes, and onion on the foil sheets and sprinkle each with ¼ teaspoon of the remaining seasoning. Top each sheet of vegetables with a meat patty and dot with the butter. Seal the foil packets tightly and transfer to a baking sheet.

3. Bake for about 30 minutes, or until the meat is cooked through and the vegetables are tender.

The Lady's House Seasoning

This is the seasoning mix we use on practically everything at The Lady & Sons. Make it up to keep in your pantry so you can add a dash of Deen to any recipe that needs a little somethin' more.

MAKES 1½ CUPS

1 cup salt
¼ cup freshly ground black pepper
¼ cup garlic powder

In a small bowl, combine the salt, pepper, and garlic powder. Transfer to an airtight container and store at room temperature for up to 6 months.

Easy Cheeseburger Casserole

We get hungry just looking at the recipe for this biscuit-topped casserole! Made with some of our favorite foods out there—ground beef, pickles, ketchup, and cheese—this casserole is a fast way to make a big family-style meal that everyone will definitely love, especially the kids.

SERVES 6 TO 8

2 tablespoons olive oil

1½ pounds ground beef

1 small onion, finely chopped

1 garlic clove, minced

1 teaspoon salt

½ teaspoon freshly ground black pepper

One 10¾-ounce can cheddar cheese soup

¾ cup diced dill pickle

3 tablespoons ketchup

3¼ cups Bisquick baking mix

1 cup milk, plus 1 to 3 tablespoons, if needed

1 cup grated extra-sharp cheddar cheese (4 ounces)

1. Preheat the oven to 400°F. Grease a 9-inch baking dish.

2. Heat 1 tablespoon of the olive oil in a large skillet over medium-high heat. Brown the beef, breaking it up with a fork, for 5 to 7 minutes, or until the meat is no longer pink. Pour off the excess drippings and use a large spoon to push the beef to the side of the pan. Add the remaining olive oil and the onion. Cook for about 5 minutes, or until the onion is translucent. Push the onion to the side with the beef. Add the garlic and cook for 30 seconds more. Stir the ingredients together and season with the salt and pepper. Stir in the cheese soup, pickle, and ketchup. Pat the mixture into the prepared baking dish.

3. In a bowl, combine the Bisquick and milk to form a dough. If the dough seems dry, stir in additional milk one tablespoon at a time. Spread evenly over the meat mixture. Scatter the cheddar cheese on top. Bake until the top is golden, about 15 minutes.

Sliced Tomato and Onion Salad with Russian Dressing

We came up with this salad, inspired by traditional burger fixin's, to eat alongside cheeseburger casserole. It's a match made in heaven. Try it with Turkey and Black Bean Burgers with Corny Salsa (page 44) or our Grilled Sausage, Pepper, and Onion Sub Sandwich (page 84).

SERVES 4 TO 6

3 tablespoons ketchup
3 tablespoons mayonnaise
2 tablespoons dill pickle relish
Salt and freshly ground black pepper to taste
3 medium beefsteak tomatoes, sliced into ¼-inch rounds
1 small red onion, very thinly sliced

1. To make the dressing: In a small bowl, mix together the ketchup, mayonnaise, pickle relish, salt, and pepper. Whisk in 1 tablespoon of water, or enough to reach a pourable consistency.

2. Arrange the tomatoes and onion on a large plate. Drizzle with the dressing before serving.

Jamie Deen's Five-Layer Beef Taco Pie

There's just something about layers of ground beef, salsa, tortilla chips, sour cream, and cheddar cheese that appeals to the soul—at least when your mama has been making seven-layer salads and dips for as long as you can remember. Mexican flavors are particularly popular for parties—Brooke is definitely a big fan of them—but this dish is quick enough to fix for a fun weeknight fiesta, too. You can use up the broken bottom-of-the-bag tortilla chips for this meal, and you don't need a side dish other than a little guacamole for dipping the extra chips in.

SERVES 4 TO 6

1½ cups crushed tortilla chips

1 tablespoon olive oil

1 pound ground beef

One 1.25-ounce packet taco seasoning mix or homemade Taco Seasoning (recipe follows)

1 cup prepared salsa, preferably fresh from your supermarket's refrigerator case

¾ cup sour cream

1 avocado, halved, peeled, pitted, and cubed

1 cup grated extra-sharp cheddar cheese (4 ounces)

1. Spray a broiler-proof 9-inch pie plate with nonstick cooking spray. Spread 1 cup of the crushed chips over the bottom of the pie plate.

2. Heat the oil in a large skillet over medium-high heat. Brown the beef, breaking it up with a fork, for 5 to 7 minutes, or until the meat is no longer pink. Pour off the drippings from the skillet and add the taco seasoning and ⅔ cup of water to the meat. Simmer, stirring occasionally, until most of the liquid has evaporated. Transfer the meat to the pie plate, spreading it on top of the chips.

3. Preheat the broiler.

4. Spread the salsa over the meat and then the sour cream over the salsa. Scatter the avocado cubes over the sour cream, and the remaining ½ cup tortilla chips over the avocado. Top with the cheddar cheese. Broil, 4 inches from the heat, for 3 to 5 minutes, or until the cheese is melted and bubbling (watch carefully to see that the cheese doesn't burn). Serve hot.

Taco Seasoning

Individual packets of taco seasoning are so convenient, but not if you have to make a special trip to the store to buy one. Here's an easy recipe you can make at home. Triple up the ingredients, if you like, so you have some extra to keep in your pantry.

MAKES 3 TABLESPOONS (EQUAL TO ¼-OUNCE TACO SEASONING PACKET)

1 tablespoon chili powder
2 teaspoons onion powder
1 teaspoon ground cumin
1 teaspoon garlic powder
1 teaspoon paprika
1 teaspoon dried oregano
1 teaspoon sugar
½ teaspoon salt

In a small bowl, combine the chili powder, onion powder, cumin, garlic powder, paprika, oregano, sugar, and salt. Use immediately or store in an airtight container at room temperature for up to 6 months.

"We're a restaurant family, but when it comes to everyday cooking, there's no place like home." —Bobby

Speedy Mini Meat Loaves

Jamie's favorite meal in the world is his wife Brooke's meat loaf. Making meat loaf in muffin pans means everyone gets his or her own, which kids always love. Of course, if you're a fan of meat loaf like Jamie is, it means you have to admit to eating two—or more—at a time. We glaze the tops with a mixture of ketchup, Worcestershire sauce, and mustard for extra flavor, but for kids, you can also serve ketchup alongside or as "frosting" on top after it comes out of the oven.

SERVES 6

1½ pounds ground beef

1 cup plain unseasoned bread crumbs

3 large eggs, lightly beaten

3 tablespoons milk

1 garlic clove, finely chopped

1 medium onion, finely chopped

1¼ teaspoons salt

1 teaspoon minced fresh thyme

¾ teaspoon freshly ground black pepper

3 tablespoons ketchup

2 tablespoons Dijon mustard

1 teaspoon Worcestershire sauce

1. Preheat the oven to 350°F. Lightly grease the cups of a 12-cup muffin pan.

2. In a large bowl, combine the beef, bread crumbs, eggs, milk, garlic, onion, salt, thyme, and pepper. Divide the meat mixture among the 12 muffin cups, pressing the meat firmly into the pan.

3. Place the muffin pan on a baking sheet and bake for 20 to 25 minutes, until the meat is almost cooked through—the "loaves" will be firm when pressed lightly in the center but not set.

4. While the meat loaves are baking, whisk together the ketchup, mustard, and Worcestershire sauce. After baking for 20 to 25 minutes, remove the pan from the oven. Brush the tops of the loaves with the glaze, using it all up, and return the pan to the oven. Bake for 10 minutes more, or until the glaze has thickened and the meat is completely cooked through, 30 to 35 minutes total. Run an offset spatula or butter knife around the edges of the muffin cups and pop out the meat loaves. Serve hot.

Roasted Sweet Potato Wedges with Brown Sugar and Cinnamon

This sweet, kid-friendly recipe (one of Jack's all-time favorites) is like a cross between candied yams and steak fries—and it's healthier than both! It's also terrific with Balsamic-Glazed London Broil (page 15) and The Ultimate Spice-Rubbed Rib Steak (page 81).

SERVES 4 TO 6

10 tablespoons unsalted butter
1½ teaspoons ground cinnamon
4 sweet potatoes, scrubbed and cut lengthwise
   into wedges
2 teaspoons salt
2 teaspoons freshly ground black pepper

1. Preheat the oven to 400°F.
2. Melt the butter in a large saucepan over medium-high heat. Remove the pan from the heat and stir in the cinnamon. Add the potato wedges and toss to combine. Season with the salt and pepper.

3. Spread the potatoes in an even layer on a baking sheet. Roast the potatoes, stirring occasionally, for 20 to 25 minutes, or until tender. Serve hot.

"Jamie and Bobby are following in our family tradition of good-looking, good-cooking men."
— Uncle Bubba

Balsamic-Glazed London Broil

London broil is a great, affordable way to serve steak to a crowd, and it's nice and thick, which makes it our favorite cut for grilling or for a sandwich the next day. Or you can slice leftovers, throw them in a pan, and make the world's best steak and eggs for breakfast. We brush the meat with balsamic vinegar, then broil it for a tangy-sweet glaze. You'll be amazed how many compliments you can get from such a simple recipe.

SERVES 6

One 3-pound London broil

½ teaspoon salt

½ teaspoon freshly ground black pepper

⅓ cup balsamic vinegar

1 tablespoon packed light brown sugar

1 garlic clove, smashed and peeled

1 bay leaf

1. Preheat the broiler. Line a rimmed baking sheet with aluminum foil.

2. Season the meat with the salt and pepper.

3. Combine the vinegar, brown sugar, garlic, and bay leaf in a large skillet. Simmer over a low heat for about 5 minutes, or until the liquid has reduced by half and is a syrupy consistency. Remove and discard the garlic and bay leaf.

4. Place the meat on the prepared baking sheet and slather with the glaze. Broil, 4 inches from the heat, turning once, to desired doneness, 12 minutes for medium-rare, up to 14 minutes for medium. Allow the meat to rest for 5 minutes, then slice very thinly, against the grain. Serve hot.

Zesty Potato, Olive, and Pimiento Salad

Potato salad always brings back good memories for us. Our dad would make it, and just as soon as the warm potatoes were tossed with the dressing, we'd all dig in. Try serving it with Roasted Spicy Mayo Chicken Breasts (page 43).

SERVES 4

2 pounds new red potatoes, halved or quartered if large
1 cup mayonnaise
1 tablespoon freshly squeezed lemon juice
1 teaspoon salt
1 teaspoon freshly ground black pepper
½ cup chopped pitted kalamata olives
½ cup chopped pimientos
¼ cup chopped fresh parsley

1. Bring a large pot of salted water to a boil. Cook the potatoes until tender, about 20 minutes. Drain well and allow to cool for five minutes.

2. In a large bowl, whisk together the mayonnaise, lemon juice, salt, and pepper. Add the potatoes, olives, pimientos, and parsley and toss to combine. Serve cold from the fridge or at room temperature.

a bit more, y'all

We think this salad tastes even better the day after it's made. Feel free to make it up in advance, or make a double batch so you can be sure there will be enough leftovers for lunch the next day.

Bobby's Favorite Beef Teriyaki Stir-fry with Broccoli and Peppers

We love how crisp and tasty the ingredients in this dish turn out when you stir-fry them. Stir-frying is a great way to make a healthy meal. And using fresh ginger adds an irresistible kick—as well as an aroma that will call everybody to the table. Put on a pot of white rice as you start cooking, and dinner will be as fast as it is flavorful.

SERVES 4

1 pound boneless beef round, cut across the grain into ½-inch-thick strips

½ cup bottled teriyaki sauce

1 tablespoon cornstarch

1 pound broccoli, cut into florets

2 tablespoons vegetable oil

1 large red bell pepper, seeded and cut into strips

2 teaspoons peeled and chopped fresh ginger

4 scallions (white and light green parts), cut into 1-inch pieces

Cooked white rice, for serving

1. In a medium bowl, combine the beef and ¼ cup of the teriyaki sauce. Cover and let marinate for at least 20 minutes and up to 4 hours. In a small bowl, combine the remaining ¼ cup teriyaki sauce and the cornstarch and stir until smooth.

2. Bring a medium pot of salted water to a boil. Cook the broccoli for 20 seconds. Drain and run the broccoli under cold water to stop the cooking. Drain well.

3. Heat 1 tablespoon of the vegetable oil in a large skillet over high heat, until a drop of water placed in the skillet sizzles. Remove the beef from the marinade and add it to the pan. Cook, stirring, for 1 to 2 minutes, or until the beef is no longer pink. Transfer the beef to a plate.

4. Wipe out the skillet and add the remaining 1 tablespoon vegetable oil. Add the red bell pepper, ginger, scallions, and broccoli and cook, stirring, for 1 minute. Add the cornstarch mixture to the pan and cook, stirring, for 2 minutes, or until it begins to thicken. Return the beef, with any accumulated juices, to the pan and cook, stirring, for 1 minute more, or until the sauce is thickened and the beef is heated through. Serve hot with the white rice.

Asian Greens and Radish Salad with Sesame Dressing

We don't use much sesame oil in our cooking, but we love how a little bit gives your whole dish a nice nutty flavor. We were playing around with trying to re-create an Asian salad dressing we had in a restaurant when we struck gold with this combo. But don't limit it to when you're cooking up Asian-inspired food. It's also great with tangy dishes like Double Orange Pork Chops (page 24) and Broiled Tuna with Pineapple-Chipotle Salsa (page 57).

SERVES 4 TO 6

3 tablespoons olive oil
1½ tablespoons rice vinegar or white wine
  vinegar
1 tablespoon sesame oil
1 garlic clove, minced
Salt and freshly ground black pepper to taste
One 5-ounce bag (about 8 cups) mixed Asian
  greens or other bagged mixed greens
1 bunch radishes, thinly sliced

1. To make the dressing: In a small bowl, whisk together the olive oil, vinegar, sesame oil, garlic, salt, and pepper.

2. In a large bowl, combine the greens and radishes. Add the dressing and toss well.

Real Easy Apple Cider Pork Tenderloin

We're big fans of pork tenderloin because it cooks pretty fast and you don't need to do much to it for it to come out meaty, satisfying, lean, and juicy all at once. Here the pork is a little sweet from the apple cider and tangy from apple cider vinegar. Roast some sweet potatoes and make a salad while the pork is cooking, and you've got a beautiful meal for the family or for company.

SERVES 4 TO 6

2 tablespoons unsalted butter

1 tablespoon olive oil

Two 1-pound pork tenderloins

1 teaspoon salt

½ teaspoon freshly ground black pepper

1 cup fresh apple cider

¼ cup apple cider vinegar

¼ teaspoon dried thyme

1. Preheat the oven to 350°F.

2. Heat the butter and olive oil in a large oven-proof skillet with a lid or in a Dutch oven over medium-high heat. Season the tenderloins with the salt and pepper. Sear the tenderloins until brown on both sides, 3 to 5 minutes per side. Add the apple cider, vinegar, and thyme and simmer, scraping up all the browned bits from the bottom of the pan.

3. Cover the pan and transfer to the oven. Cook, turning once after 10 minutes. Cook for 10 minutes more, or until an instant-read thermometer inserted into the thickest part of the meat registers 150°F.

4. Transfer the pork to a platter and cover loosely with aluminum foil. Put the skillet with the cider juices on the stove over high heat and cook until the liquid is slightly thickened and reduced to ½ cup, 5 to 7 minutes. Slice the pork and serve with the sauce spooned over.

Garlic Mashed Potatoes

This is our go-to side dish for any and every recipe that gives you good gravy. Yukon Gold potatoes make a nice sweet, creamy mash. Try it with Bobby's Turkey Vegetable Goulash (page 132) or Baked Chicken with Zucchini and Herbs (page 37).

SERVES 6

2½ pounds Yukon Gold potatoes, peeled
1 cup milk
1 tablespoon chopped garlic
6 tablespoons unsalted butter
1½ teaspoons salt, plus additional to taste
Freshly ground black pepper to taste

1. Bring a large pot of salted water to a boil.

Cook the potatoes until tender, about 25 minutes. Drain well.

2. Combine the milk and garlic in a saucepan and simmer for 5 minutes.

3. In a large bowl, mash the potatoes, milk mixture, butter, salt, and pepper to the desired consistency. Taste and adjust the seasonings, if necessary. Serve immediately.

Smothered Pork Chops and Rice Bake

We hadn't had Mama's pork chops and rice bake in years when Bobby—who is on a pork chop kick—decided it was worth reviving. We brown the chops like Mama taught us, to give them a really rich flavor and seal in the juices. Then we smother them in cheese, which is our own addition to Mama's classic recipe, and bake them with cream of chicken soup and rice for one of the most luscious one-pot suppers ever. We make a version of this at The Lady & Sons, where it's a real crowd-pleaser.

SERVES 4

1 tablespoon vegetable oil

Four 8-ounce center-cut, bone-in pork loin chops, ½ inch thick

½ teaspoon salt

½ teaspoon freshly ground black pepper

¾ cup uncooked long-grain rice

One 10¾-ounce can condensed cream of chicken soup

2 cups grated cheddar cheese (8 ounces)

⅓ cup finely chopped Vidalia onion or scallions (white and light green parts)

1. Preheat the oven to 375°F.

2. Heat the vegetable oil in an ovenproof skillet with a lid over medium-high heat. Season the pork chops with the salt and pepper. Cook, turning once, until brown on both sides, 6 to 8 minutes total.

3. Meanwhile, in a bowl, mix together ¼ cup of water, the rice, cream of chicken soup, and cheddar cheese.

4. When the chops are browned, add the rice mixture to the skillet. Cover and transfer to the oven. Bake for 45 minutes, or until the rice is done. Scatter the onion over the top and serve.

"Canned cream of whatever soup is the fixin' to a great meal, just waiting to jump off the shelf."
—Jamie

Italian-Style Pork Chops

Southern cooks love to serve Swiss steak—a dish made with a tougher cut of beef that's been pounded and braised with enough red sauce that it becomes so tender you can eat it without a knife. And that's where the idea for this dish came from—pork chops cooked in marinara sauce and topped with cheese. We like to serve the chops with a bowl of egg noodles tossed with butter and chopped fresh parsley or with our Garlic Mashed Potatoes (page 21)—anything to soak up some of the delicious sauce.

SERVES 4

1 tablespoon olive oil

Four 8-ounce center-cut, boneless pork loin chops, ½ inch thick

¼ teaspoon salt

¼ teaspoon freshly ground black pepper

2 cups prepared marinara sauce

2 cups shredded mozzarella (8 ounces)

¼ teaspoon dried oregano

1. Heat the olive oil in a large skillet with a lid over medium-high heat. Season the pork with the salt and pepper. Cook, turning once, until brown on both sides, 6 to 8 minutes total.

2. Pour the marinara sauce into the skillet and bring to a boil, turning the chops a few times. Reduce the heat to medium, cover the pan, and cook for 5 minutes. Turn the chops over and scatter the mozzarella and oregano on top. Cover again and cook until the cheese is melted and the pork is just cooked through, 4 to 5 minutes more.

Double Orange Pork Chops

PHOTOGRAPH ON PAGE xxii

We do so many pork chops at home and at The Lady & Sons these days because they're fast—you can make as many as you need—and they're a good change from red meat or chicken. This recipe is a really nice way to enjoy them. Orange marmalade gives them a sweetness that's perfect for adding a little zest to your meal.

SERVES 4

1 cup freshly squeezed orange juice

⅓ cup orange marmalade

3 tablespoons unsalted butter

1 tablespoon vegetable oil

Four 8-ounce center-cut, bone-in pork loin chops, ½ inch thick

1 teaspoon salt

¼ teaspoon freshly ground black pepper

1. In a small bowl, mix together the orange juice and marmalade.

2. Heat the butter and vegetable oil in a large skillet over medium heat. Season the pork chops with the salt and pepper. Cook, turning once, until just cooked through, 6 to 8 minutes total. Transfer the chops to a platter and cover loosely with aluminum foil.

3. Pour off all but 3 tablespoons of drippings from the skillet and add the orange juice mixture. Raise the heat to medium-high and stir, scraping up the brown bits on the bottom of the pan, until the sauce is reduced and slightly syrupy, 6 to 8 minutes. Return the pork chops to the pan, reduce the heat to medium, and cook, turning the pork chops a few times in the sauce.

4. Drizzle the pork chops with some of the sauce and pass the remaining sauce in a bowl.

Buttery Stone-Ground Grits

We're not too modest to say that we've perfected the quintessential Southern bowl of supercreamy grits. Try this for breakfast with fried eggs and ham or serve it with Sautéed Shrimp with Bacon and Mushrooms (page 67) or Sweet and Spicy Pork (page 128).

SERVES 6

1 cup stone-ground or old-fashioned grits
1 teaspoon salt, plus additional to taste
6 tablespoons unsalted butter, cubed
¾ cup heavy cream

1. Bring 4 cups of water to a boil in a medium pot. Slowly add the grits, stirring constantly to avoid lumps.

2. Add the salt and partially cover. Reduce the heat to medium and cook for 15 minutes, stirring occasionally.

3. Uncover the pot and stir in the butter and 3 tablespoons of the cream. Continue to stir, adding cream a few tablespoons at a time once the mixture thickens and begins to sputter slightly. Add the cream until all of it has been combined, about 15 minutes more. Taste and add more salt, if desired.

poultry

BROILED PESTO CHICKEN WITH CHERRY TOMATOES 30

CREAMY CHICKEN ALFREDO BAKE 32

Tomato and Mozzarella Salad with Balsamic Vinegar and Basil 32

HONEY MUSTARD BAKED CHICKEN 33

Warm Macaroni and Mozzarella Salad with Herbs 33

QUICK BRAISED CHICKEN WITH ROSEMARY AND POTATOES 35

Crunchy Iceberg Lettuce Salad with Blue Cheese Dressing 35

CHICKEN AND VEGGIE STIR-FRY WITH SPICY SOY SAUCE 36

BAKED CHICKEN WITH ZUCCHINI AND HERBS 37

GARLICKY CHICKEN AND PEANUT STIR-FRY 38

Avocado and Carrot Salad with Sesame Dressing 40

GRANNY'S FRIED CHICKEN 41

ROASTED SPICY MAYO CHICKEN BREASTS 43

Sautéed Spinach and Onions 43

TURKEY AND BLACK BEAN BURGERS WITH CORNY SALSA 44

Moist-and-Easy Corn Bread 45

PEPPERY TURKEY SCALOPPINI 46

Easy Almond Rice Pilaf 47

SOUTHERN-STYLE TURKEY, TOMATO, AND MONTEREY JACK BAKE 48

Bobby's Tasty Steamed Broccoli with Garlic 48

We owe Mr. Chicken a great deal of thanks. When we were kids, it seemed like we had chicken all the time. Mom cut up a lot of fryers, and her fried chicken has always been the heart and soul of The Lady & Sons. Plus, chicken is one of the foods Jamie's son, Jack, will almost always eat if all else fails. Once you have a child, you start to really appreciate the foods that bring the whole family together.

We've been cooking with turkey a lot more these days, too, since it's not too filling and it has a nice, rich flavor and great texture. We're big fans of Italian food, and we consider turkey a great alternative to veal in recipes like **Peppery Turkey Scaloppini** (page 46). And on nights when we're trying to take a break from red meat, ground turkey is a satisfying base for burgers. All in all, we just decided one day that turkey is way too good to wait until November to eat, so we've been finding ways to use it in more everyday recipes.

Poultry is one of the fastest ways to get everyone fed well, especially if you're baking or stir-frying it. We love how it takes on different flavors, so with seasonings you can go in any direction you like, whether you're craving something like the Thai flavors of **Garlicky Chicken and Peanut Stir-fry** (page 38) or the Italian taste of **Creamy Chicken Alfredo Bake** (page 32). And you don't need to plan ahead to create a healthy, beautiful dinner with a dish like **Quick Braised Chicken with Rosemary and Potatoes** (page 35). Fix a salad while the chicken is in the oven, and you've got a meal you could serve company.

If you're still not convinced that chicken and turkey are the best things to happen to weeknights since ESPN, try our **Honey Mustard Baked Chicken** (page 33). It's our current favorite way to enjoy chicken, and we're pretty sure it'll convince you, too.

Broiled Pesto Chicken with Cherry Tomatoes

In his late twenties, Jamie spent a lot of time eating at his favorite pizza place in Savannah, called Cousin Vinny's. He became obsessed with their pesto pizza, which uses savory basil sauce in place of the usual tomato. We don't eat quite as much pizza these days, but we do keep pesto in our freezers for whenever we want fresh garlic and basil flavor. Try tossing pesto with cherry tomatoes and leftover grilled chicken and serve it on top of greens for a main-course salad, or make this easy, healthy recipe, which takes about fifteen minutes and looks as good as it tastes. For a little decadence, try serving it with Cheesy Garlic Bread (page 102).

SERVES 4

1 pint cherry tomatoes

¼ cup prepared pesto sauce, preferably fresh from your supermarket's refrigerator case

Salt and freshly ground black pepper to taste

4 boneless skinless chicken breast halves

1. Preheat the oven to 450°F. Lightly coat a baking pan with nonstick cooking spray.

2. In a bowl, toss the cherry tomatoes with 1 tablespoon of the pesto and season with salt and pepper. Coat the chicken breasts with the remaining 3 tablespoons pesto and season with additional salt, if desired.

3. Arrange the chicken in the prepared baking pan. Bake for 10 minutes. Add the tomatoes and bake for 10 more minutes, or until the juices run clear when the chicken is pricked with a fork.

a bit more, y'all

Pestos vary in their salt content, so take a little taste of the pesto before it goes on the chicken and season accordingly.

Creamy Chicken Alfredo Bake

We try to eat a healthy, balanced diet, but you know Paula Deen's boys have a taste for rich, creamy sauces. One of our favorite foods in a jar is Alfredo sauce, and it's the perfect base for the world's fastest chicken and pasta casserole. We throw in peas for a little green color, and add a nice tomato salad to get our veggies in.

SERVES 4 TO 6

8 ounces (2 cups) penne pasta

One 10-ounce package frozen peas

4 cups shredded cooked chicken

One 15-ounce jar Alfredo sauce

1 cup grated Parmesan cheese (4 ounces)

1. Preheat the oven to 375°F. Butter a 9 x 13-inch baking dish.

2. Bring a large pot of salted water to a boil. Cook the penne for 7 to 9 minutes. When the penne is almost done (firm but no longer crunchy), add the peas and continue cooking for 1 minute more. Reserve ¼ cup of the cooking water and drain the penne and peas.

3. In a large bowl, combine the penne, peas, chicken, Alfredo sauce, and the reserved pasta cooking water. Transfer the mixture to the prepared baking dish and top with the Parmesan cheese. Bake for 20 minutes, or until the cheese is melted and browned at the edges.

Tomato and Mozzarella Salad with Balsamic Vinegar and Basil

Who doesn't love this combo? You can pay twenty bucks to eat it all nicely stacked up at a five-star restaurant, or you can make it at home for a lot less, and it'll be just as good. Try it with any Italian-accented dish, like Braised Chicken with Peppers and Mushrooms (page 129) or Creamy, Spicy Sausage Pasta (page 105).

SERVES 4

1 pound medium vine-ripened tomatoes, cut into chunks
2 cups cubed mozzarella (8 ounces)
3 tablespoons chopped fresh basil
2 tablespoons olive oil
1 tablespoon balsamic vinegar
Salt and freshly ground black pepper to taste

In a large bowl, toss together the tomatoes, mozzarella, basil, olive oil, vinegar, salt, and pepper. Let stand for 10 minutes at room temperature before serving.

Honey Mustard Baked Chicken

We perfected making honey mustard during the early days at The Lady & Sons, where it's served mostly on the side as a condiment, or as a dipping sauce for the kids' menu (see The Lady & Sons Honey Mustard Sauce, page 159). At home, we throw store-bought honey mustard in with chicken for this family-pleasing dish that's a little sweet on the outside and nice and juicy inside. Warm macaroni and mozzarella salad is a nice complement to the chicken.

SERVES 4

3 tablespoons honey mustard

1 tablespoon olive oil

1 teaspoon tomato paste

4 boneless skinless chicken breast halves

Salt and freshly ground black pepper to taste

1. Preheat the oven to 400°F. Line a rimmed baking sheet with aluminum foil.

2. In a small bowl, whisk together the honey mustard, olive oil, and tomato paste.

3. Season the chicken with salt and pepper. Slather the honey mustard glaze over the chicken.

4. Arrange the chicken on the prepared sheet. Bake for about 25 minutes, or until golden and the juices run clear when the chicken is pricked with a fork.

Warm Macaroni and Mozzarella Salad with Herbs

Macaroni salad is all over the South. This is our refreshing Italian-inspired take on the usual mayonnaise-based kind. You can toss in leftover grilled chicken for a main-course salad. Kids tend to love macaroni, so we leave out the herbs when we know we're feeding someone who isn't a fan of "green bits." Try it next time you serve up Chicken Nuggets with Honey-Lemon Dipping Sauce (page 159) or our Saucy Tilapia with Tomatoes and Capers (page 56).

SERVES 4 TO 6

8 ounces (2 cups) macaroni
2 tablespoons olive oil
2 teaspoons red wine vinegar
2 teaspoons freshly squeezed lemon juice
Salt and freshly ground black pepper to taste
½ cup chopped fresh basil
1 tablespoon chopped fresh oregano, thyme, or parsley or 1 teaspoon dried oregano, thyme, or parsley
2 cups shredded mozzarella (8 ounces)

1. Bring a large pot of salted water to a boil. Cook the macaroni according to the package directions.

2. Meanwhile, to make the dressing: In a small bowl, whisk together the olive oil, vinegar, lemon juice, salt, and pepper.

3. Drain the macaroni and transfer to a medium bowl. Add the basil and oregano and half of the dressing. Stir to combine. Let sit for 1 minute to cool slightly, then add the mozzarella and the remaining dressing. Serve warm.

Quick Braised Chicken with Rosemary and Potatoes

Drumsticks are always our favorite, but Mama always likes the thighs, so we make it so that everyone can get what they want. Rosemary really complements the new red potatoes and gives them a hearty garden flavor, and using dark meat keeps the dish juicy. We love this with a light side salad like our crunchy iceberg lettuce salad with blue cheese.

SERVES 4 TO 6

2 teaspoons salt, plus additional for seasoning

1 teaspoon freshly ground black pepper, plus additional for seasoning

3 tablespoons olive oil

2 garlic cloves, minced

1½ tablespoons freshly squeezed lemon juice

1 tablespoon chopped fresh rosemary or 1 teaspoon dried rosemary

3 pounds chicken legs, cut into thighs and drumsticks (or just use one or the other)

1 pound small new red potatoes, cut into eighths

1. Preheat the oven to 400°F.

2. In a small bowl, whisk together the 2 teaspoons salt, 1 teaspoon pepper, the olive oil, garlic, lemon juice, and rosemary.

3. Place the chicken in a large broiler-proof baking pan and season with the additional salt and pepper. Add the potatoes to the pan. Pour the rosemary mixture over the chicken and potatoes and toss to coat.

4. Cover the pan with aluminum foil and bake for 30 minutes. Uncover the pan and transfer to the broiler. Broil, 4 inches from the heat, for 5 to 10 minutes, or until the juices run clear when the chicken is pricked with a fork. Serve hot, with the pan juices spooned on top.

Crunchy Iceberg Lettuce Salad with Blue Cheese Dressing

You can transform this perfect crisp side salad into a main-course salad by slicing up any meat you like and tossing it on top. Or try it alongside Grilled Caesar Pork Tenderloin (page 89) or Down-Home Pinto Beans and Ham Hocks (page 127).

SERVES 4

1 cup crumbled blue cheese (4 ounces)
¼ cup sour cream
¼ cup olive oil
Salt and freshly ground black pepper to taste
6 cups chopped iceberg lettuce (½ large head)

1. To make the dressing: In a small bowl, whisk together ¼ cup of the blue cheese, the sour cream, olive oil, salt, and pepper.

2. In a large bowl, combine the lettuce and the remaining ¾ cup blue cheese. Toss with the dressing and serve.

Chicken and Veggie Stir-fry with Spicy Soy Sauce

Serve this lean, veggie-heavy stir-fry with white rice to sop up the delicious Tabasco-spiked soy sauce.

SERVES 4

¼ cup chicken broth

3 tablespoons soy sauce

1 tablespoon cornstarch

1 teaspoon sesame oil

¾ teaspoon Tabasco or other hot sauce

1 tablespoon vegetable oil

2 boneless skinless chicken breast halves, cut crosswise into ½-inch strips

¼ pound snow peas, trimmed

1 red bell pepper, halved lengthwise, seeded, and cut crosswise into ¼-inch strips

One 15-ounce can straw mushrooms

Cooked white rice, for serving

1. To make the sauce: In a small bowl, combine the chicken broth, soy sauce, cornstarch, sesame oil, and Tabasco and stir until smooth.

2. Heat the vegetable oil in a large nonstick skillet over high heat until a drop of water placed in the skillet sizzles. Add the chicken strips and cook, stirring, for 3 to 4 minutes, or until they lose their raw color. Add the snow peas and cook, stirring, for 1 minute. Add the bell pepper strips and cook, stirring, for 2 minutes. Add the mushrooms and soy sauce mixture and cook, stirring, for 2 to 3 minutes, or until the sauce is thickened. Serve hot with the white rice.

a bit more, y'all

We use snow peas, bell pepper, and canned straw mushrooms here, but you can use anything you've got instead. Broccoli florets, sugar snaps, string beans, or sliced carrots work nicely.

Baked Chicken with Zucchini and Herbs

Baking chicken on top of zucchini is a great way to get your green vegetables in. The zucchini absorbs all the chicken and herb flavors in the pan and winds up tasting a whole lot better than any vegetable really should. We love to bake chicken pieces with a slice of lemon on top because the lemon browns right along with the chicken skin and adds a nice zesty flavor.

SERVES 4

2 medium zucchini (about 1½ pounds), cut into ¼-inch-thick slices

1¾ teaspoons salt

1½ teaspoons freshly ground black pepper

1 teaspoon dried thyme

1 teaspoon dried oregano

1½ pounds boneless skinless chicken thighs

2 tablespoons unsalted butter, cubed

½ teaspoon freshly squeezed lime juice, plus lime wedges, for serving

1½ lemons, very thinly sliced

1. Preheat the oven to 425°F.

2. Arrange the zucchini slices in a single layer in a large roasting pan. Season with ½ teaspoon each of the salt, pepper, thyme, and oregano.

3. Season the chicken with the remaining 1¼ teaspoons salt and the remaining 1 teaspoon pepper. Arrange the chicken on top of the zucchini, leaving space for air to circulate. Scatter the butter over the chicken and zucchini. Season with the remaining thyme and the remaining oregano. Drizzle with the lime juice. Arrange the lemon slices over the chicken.

4. Bake, basting once about halfway through, for about 25 minutes, or until the zucchini is tender and the chicken is lightly browned and the juices run clear when it is pricked with a fork. Serve hot with the lime wedges.

Garlicky Chicken and Peanut Stir-fry

We can get behind any recipe with peanut butter in it! This savory dish, with just a hint of fiery red pepper flakes, is a nod to our favorite Thai take-out dish from Kao Thai in Savannah. Best of all, it's based on ingredients you probably already have in the house.

SERVES 4 TO 6

6 tablespoons creamy peanut butter

1 tablespoon packed dark brown sugar

1½ tablespoons soy sauce

Freshly squeezed juice of 1 lime, plus lime wedges, for serving

½ teaspoon crushed red pepper flakes or to taste

4 boneless skinless chicken breast halves, cut crosswise into 2-inch strips

Salt and freshly ground black pepper to taste

2 tablespoons peanut or vegetable oil

6 tablespoons thinly sliced scallions (white and light green parts)

2 tablespoons finely chopped garlic

2 tablespoons peeled and finely chopped fresh ginger

Cooked white rice, for serving

1. Whisk together the peanut butter, brown sugar, soy sauce, lime juice, red pepper flakes, and ½ cup of water in a saucepan over medium-low heat. Cook for 5 to 7 minutes, stirring constantly, until the sauce is smooth and completely warmed through.

2. Season the chicken with salt and pepper. Heat the peanut oil in a very large skillet over medium heat. Cook the chicken, stirring occasionally, for 5 to 7 minutes, or until golden and the juices run clear when the chicken is pricked with a fork. Add the scallions, garlic, and ginger and cook for 1 minute more.

3. Remove the skillet from the heat, pour in the peanut butter mixture, and toss with the chicken. Serve hot with the white rice.

Avocado and Carrot Salad with Sesame Dressing

This salad looks almost too pretty to eat! Try it with other Asian-inspired dishes like Broiled Tuna with Pineapple-Chipotle Salsa (page 57) or Bobby's Favorite Beef Teriyaki Stir-fry with Broccoli and Peppers (page 18).

SERVES 4 TO 6

6 tablespoons peanut oil

¼ cup soy sauce

2 tablespoons sesame oil

2 tablespoons freshly squeezed lime juice

2 avocados, halved, peeled, pitted, and cubed

1 pound carrots, peeled and grated (about 4 cups)

½ cup chopped fresh cilantro

1. To make the dressing: In a small bowl, whisk together the peanut oil, soy sauce, sesame oil, and lime juice.

2. In a large bowl, combine the avocados, carrots, and cilantro. Toss with the dressing before serving.

"Honey, you know I love the nice, juicy dark meat. I had better, after raising two breast-meat boys!" —Paula

Granny's Fried Chicken

PHOTOGRAPH ON PAGE 28

This is our Granny Paul's recipe for fried chicken, and it's as simple a taste of Southern home cooking as there ever could be. Serve it with collard greens and some mashed potatoes, and before you know it you'll be whistlin' "Dixie." And you don't need to save this meal for Sunday suppers—if you're short on time, just skip the refrigeration and season the chicken right before you fry it to have yourself a down-home after-work treat.

SERVES 4 TO 6

One 3½- to 4-pound fryer chicken, cut into 8 pieces

Salt and pepper to taste

4 large eggs

1 tablespoon Tabasco or other hot sauce

2 cups all-purpose flour

4 cups peanut oil, for frying

1. Season the chicken generously with the salt and pepper. Cover the chicken and refrigerate for at least 3 hours and up to 8 hours.

2. In a medium bowl, whisk together the eggs and Tabasco sauce. Place the flour in a separate bowl.

3. Pour the oil ½ inch deep into a 12-inch cast-iron or heavy-bottomed skillet and heat over a medium flame until the oil measures 350° on a candy thermometer.

4. Starting with the 4 pieces of dark meat, dredge the chicken in the egg mixture, then coat in the flour, shaking off any excess. Place the pieces in the oil and fry, turning often, for 12 to 15 minutes, or until the juices run clear. Transfer the chicken to a paper-towel-lined plate to drain. Repeat with the 4 pieces of white meat, and fry, turning often, for 10 to 12 minutes, or until the juices run clear. Transfer to a paper-towel-lined plate to drain. Serve immediately.

Roasted Spicy Mayo Chicken Breasts

Coating chicken with mayonnaise and spices before you bake it not only makes for a beautifully browned outside, it also helps bring out the flavor of your seasonings. We use the same technique for our beer-in-the-rear whole chicken on the grill. But chicken breasts cook up faster, and this preparation couldn't be simpler.

SERVES 4

½ cup mayonnaise

Finely grated zest of 2 lemons

2 teaspoons paprika

¾ teaspoon celery seeds

1 teaspoon salt, plus additional for seasoning

1 teaspoon freshly ground black pepper, plus additional for seasoning

Pinch of cayenne pepper

4 boneless skinless chicken breast halves

1. Preheat the oven to 425°F. Line a rimmed baking sheet with aluminum foil.

2. In a small bowl, whisk together the mayonnaise, lemon zest, paprika, celery seeds, the 1 teaspoon salt, the 1 teaspoon pepper, and the cayenne.

3. Season the chicken with the additional salt and pepper. Arrange the chicken on the prepared sheet. Slather the mayonnaise mixture over the chicken. Bake for 20 to 25 minutes, or until the juices run clear when the chicken is pricked with a fork. Serve hot.

Sautéed Spinach and Onions

This is one of the fastest, tastiest ways you can serve spinach. We probably make it a few times a month. Just start tossing a bag of spinach into the shopping cart every week and you'll see what we mean. This side also goes great with Smothered Pork Chops and Rice Bake (page 22) and Pecan Catfish Fish Sticks (page 160).

SERVES 4

3 tablespoons unsalted butter

1 small onion, halved and thinly sliced

One 9-ounce bag (about 14 cups) baby spinach

¾ teaspoon The Lady's House Seasoning (page 7)

½ teaspoon freshly squeezed lemon juice, or more to taste

1. Melt the butter in a skillet over medium heat. Add the onion and cook for 3 to 5 minutes, or until softened.

2. Add the spinach. Toss to wilt, about 1 minute. Sprinkle on the house seasoning and lemon juice and serve.

Turkey and Black Bean Burgers with Corny Salsa

PHOTOGRAPH ON PAGE 26

Can you guess how many turkey-bean burgers we ate when we were growing up? Zero! We're big beef burger fans and we could eat a burger every few nights if we let ourselves. So every now and then, we lighten things up with turkey and black beans in this Mexican-inspired twist on a traditional burger. It's about as healthy a burger as you could ask for, and it's a real crowd-pleaser, too—even little Jack likes it! And since we usually serve this burger without the bun, we like to make our corn bread to go with it.

SERVES 6 TO 8

1¼ pounds ground turkey

One 15-ounce can black beans, rinsed, drained, and lightly mashed

½ cup crushed tortilla chips

2 teaspoons The Lady's House Seasoning (page 7)

1 tablespoon chili powder

1 teaspoon ground cumin

¼ cup olive oil

1 cup prepared salsa, preferably fresh from your supermarket's refrigerator case

1 cup frozen corn kernels, thawed

1 avocado, halved, peeled, pitted, and finely diced

Sour cream, for serving

1. In a large bowl, combine the turkey, beans, tortilla chips, house seasoning, chili powder, and cumin. Use your hands to form the mixture into 8 equal-size patties.

2. Heat the olive oil in a large skillet over medium-high heat. Working in batches, if necessary, cook the patties for 4 to 5 minutes per side, or until no longer pink in the middle. Transfer the patties to a paper-towel-lined plate to drain.

3. In a small bowl, mix together the salsa, corn, and avocado. Spoon the salsa mixture over the burgers and top with sour cream to serve.

Moist-and-Easy Corn Bread

Not too sweet and just moist enough—this corn bread goes with anything! Try it with Spicy Oven-Baked Pepper Shrimp (page 69) and All-Day Beef Chili (page 122).

SERVES 4 TO 6

1 cup cornmeal
¾ cup all-purpose flour
3 tablespoons sugar
1½ teaspoons baking powder
½ teaspoon baking soda
¼ teaspoon salt
2 large eggs, lightly beaten
1½ cups buttermilk
6 tablespoons unsalted butter, melted

1. Preheat the oven to 425°F. Lightly grease an 8-inch baking dish.

2. In a large bowl, mix together the cornmeal, flour, sugar, baking powder, baking soda, and salt.

3. In a separate bowl, mix together the eggs, buttermilk, and butter. Pour the buttermilk mixture into the cornmeal mixture and fold together until there are no dry spots (the batter will still be lumpy). Pour the batter into the prepared baking dish.

4. Bake for 20 to 25 minutes, or until the top is golden and a tester inserted into the middle of the corn bread comes out clean. Allow the corn bread to cool for 10 minutes before serving.

Peppery Turkey Scaloppini

We love the sweet-sour taste of classic veal scaloppini, but we have started using turkey cutlets in our peppery version. Turkey has such a rich taste, plus it's leaner and less expensive than veal. This recipe is simple enough for everyday dinners, but it tastes special enough that you can eat it by candlelight, especially when it's served with our almond rice pilaf.

SERVES 4

1 tablespoon olive oil

5 tablespoons unsalted butter

1 medium onion, chopped

Four 6-ounce turkey cutlets

1 teaspoon salt

1 teaspoon freshly ground
   black pepper

½ cup chicken broth

3 tablespoons red wine vinegar

1. Heat the olive oil and 2 tablespoons of the butter in a large skillet over medium heat. Add the onion and cook, stirring occasionally, for 3 to 5 minutes, or until softened. Push the onion to the side of the pan and add 1 more tablespoon of the butter.

2. Season the turkey with the salt and ½ teaspoon of the pepper and add to the pan. Turn the heat up to medium-high and cook the turkey until browned on both sides, about 4 minutes total. Transfer the turkey to a platter and cover loosely with aluminum foil.

3. Add the chicken broth, vinegar, and the remaining ½ teaspoon pepper to the pan with the onion. Turn the heat up to high and simmer until the liquid is reduced by half, 5 to 7 minutes. Reduce the heat to medium and whisk in the remaining 2 tablespoons butter, 1 tablespoon at a time. Return the turkey, along with any accumulated juices, to the skillet and cook, turning occasionally, until cooked through, about 1 minute.

a bit more, y'all

If you can adjust your pepper mill, the more coarsely ground the pepper, the better for this sauce.

Easy Almond Rice Pilaf

Just like every guy needs a great-fitting sport coat, every cook needs a fast way to dress up rice. You can play around with this recipe: Add pine nuts and basil in place of the almonds and parsley, use basmati rice, whatever floats your boat. It's also terrific with pork, so think of it next time you cook up Double Orange Pork Chops (page 24) or Bobby's Special Thick-Cut Garlic Pork Chops with Bourbon Glaze (page 87).

SERVES 6

3 tablespoons unsalted butter
1 medium onion, finely chopped
1½ cups uncooked long-grain rice
2 cups chicken broth
1½ teaspoons salt
1 cup slivered almonds, toasted
3 tablespoons chopped fresh parsley
¼ teaspoon freshly ground black pepper

1. Melt the butter in a saucepan over medium heat. Add the onion and cook 3 to 5 minutes, or until softened. Stir in the rice and cook for 1 minute more. Stir in the chicken broth, 1 cup of water, and the salt.

2. Reduce the heat to medium-low. Cover the saucepan and simmer for 17 minutes, or until the rice is tender and all the water is absorbed. Add the almonds, parsley, and pepper, and fluff to combine.

Southern-Style Turkey, Tomato, and Monterey Jack Bake

If you've ever had Frito pie down South, then you know where we're coming from here. This creamy turkey casserole, topped with a crispy layer of melted cheese and crushed corn chips, is the kind of thing that can make grown men cry on Super Bowl Sunday. Bobby loves to serve this with a side of crunchy, garlicky broccoli.

SERVES 4

2 tablespoons vegetable oil

1 pound ground turkey

1 medium onion, chopped

One 10¾-ounce can condensed Southwestern pepper Jack or cream of celery soup

1 cup canned diced tomatoes

1 cup frozen corn kernels, thawed

2 cups grated Monterey Jack cheese (8 ounces)

2 cups crushed corn chips

1. Preheat the oven to 400°F.

2. Heat the vegetable oil in a medium ovenproof skillet over medium-high heat. Add the turkey and onion and cook, stirring frequently, until no pink remains in the meat, about 5 minutes. Add the pepper Jack soup, tomatoes, and corn and bring to a boil. Cook, stirring frequently, for 5 minutes.

3. Remove the skillet from the heat and top the turkey mixture with the Monterey Jack cheese and corn chips. Transfer to the oven and bake for 10 minutes, or until the cheese is melted and the casserole is bubbly. Serve immediately.

Bobby's Tasty Steamed Broccoli with Garlic

Folks love this recipe, whether or not they're broccoli fans. It's dressed like a salad, with a nice little tang from the vinegar. It adds something green and healthy to meaty mains like this one, and we also love it with Mama's Hamburger "Hobo Sacks" (page 7) and Smothered Pork Chops and Rice Bake (page 22).

SERVES 4

2 tablespoons olive oil
1½ teaspoons red wine vinegar
1 garlic clove, minced
½ teaspoon salt
½ teaspoon freshly ground black pepper
1 pound broccoli, cut into bite-size florets

1. To make the dressing: In a small bowl, whisk together the olive oil, vinegar, garlic, salt, and pepper.

2. Using a steamer basket over a large pot of boiling water, steam the broccoli for 5 to 7 minutes, or until tender. Transfer the broccoli to a serving bowl. Pour the dressing over the broccoli and toss to combine.

fish

BAKED SALMON WITH LEMONY MAYO 54

Baby Lettuce and Cucumber Salad 54

SAUCY TILAPIA WITH TOMATOES AND CAPERS 56

BROILED TUNA WITH PINEAPPLE-CHIPOTLE SALSA 57

SEARED RED SNAPPER WITH ZESTY BASIL BUTTER 58

Couscous with Mushrooms 60

BAKED TROUT WITH LEMON AND ROSEMARY 61

Green Beans with Black Olives 61

NOT-YOUR-MAMA'S TUNA CASSEROLE 62

shrimp

JERK SHRIMP KEBABS WITH TOMATOES, ONIONS, AND PEPPERS 64

Coconut-Orange Cashew Rice 66

SAUTÉED SHRIMP WITH BACON AND MUSHROOMS 67

Vidalia-Onion-Stuffed Baked Potatoes with "The Deens' List" of Toppings 68

SPICY OVEN-BAKED PEPPER SHRIMP 69

SHRIMP 'N' GRITS 70

BUTTER-BRAISED SHRIMP 72

Growing up in Albany in the southwest corner of Georgia, we were pretty landlocked. But from a young age we always loved freshwater fishing, even if we didn't particularly care for eating those scrawny fish once they were fried up (well, Jamie remembers enjoying the tartar sauce). Now that we live in Savannah, we have access to all kinds of fresh seafood right in our backyards, and we are a fish's worst enemy. Even Jack has a little fishing rod, and Mama nets shrimp and blue crabs fairly often, too.

We love fishing, but we also love how convenient it is to build a week-night supper around fresh fish from the market. You can just pick it up after work, bring it home, put it in a pan with some butter, lemon, and seasonings, and you have your meal. Plus it's so versatile—feel free to swap in similar styles of fish in any recipe (pollack in place of tilapia, halibut for tuna, and, because they're so abundant down here, catfish in place of anything). The key is to take advantage of what's fresh and on sale at your local market.

Since fish is so light tasting, it's easy to pair it with sauces and sides, whether you want to do something comfortingly familiar like **Baked Salmon with Lemony Mayo** (page 54), or something a little more out of the box like **Saucy Tilapia with Tomatoes and Capers** (page 56), which is great with couscous or pasta.

Once you bring home some good-quality fresh fish or seafood, the only real task is to cook it quickly, until it's slightly firm and just cooked through. Overcooked seafood gets fishy tasting and loses its nice texture. Of course, there's an even simpler option, which we're big fans of: canned fish. It's bone free, cooked for you, fresh in your pantry whenever you need it, and affordable. Don't save those cans for sandwiches only. Instead, break out **Not-Your-Mama's Tuna Casserole** (page 62). Kids who think fish is a bit "fishy" won't turn down a casserole with noodles and corn in it, and we've never met a grown-up who didn't have seconds.

Baked Salmon with Lemony Mayo

Salmon is something so healthy that we just had to put mayonnaise on it. The lemon mayo gives it a great zesty flavor and oomph—it keeps the fish moist, too. Our lettuce and cucumber salad is a perfect match for this light dish.

SERVES 4

½ cup mayonnaise

2 tablespoons finely grated lemon zest

2 teaspoons finely chopped garlic

1 teaspoon Tabasco or other hot sauce

Four 8-ounce salmon fillets

Salt and freshly ground black pepper to taste

1. Preheat the oven to 425°F. Line a rimmed baking sheet with aluminum foil.

2. In a medium bowl, whisk together the mayonnaise, lemon zest, garlic, and Tabasco.

3. Season the salmon fillets with salt and pepper and place them on the prepared baking sheet. Slather the mayonnaise mixture over the salmon.

4. Transfer the sheet to the oven and bake for 8 to 10 minutes, or until the salmon just flakes with a fork.

a bit more, y'all

For a lighter dish, you can use reduced-fat mayonnaise. Also try adding a sprinkling of chopped dill for even more fresh flavor.

Baby Lettuce and Cucumber Salad

When we were kids, just a little older than Jack is now, we used to run over to Granny Paul's house to pick the baby lettuce in her spring garden. Now we can find bagged conveniently baby lettuce in our supermarket. We like to make this salad to accompany and lighten up all kinds of heartier fare, like Creamy Chicken Alfredo Bake (page 32). If you can't get baby lettuce, you can make this recipe with any kind of lettuce you've got in the fridge.

SERVES 4

2 tablespoons white wine vinegar
2 tablespoons chopped fresh dill
Salt and freshly ground black pepper to taste
¼ cup vegetable oil
6 cups (about 4 ounces) baby lettuce or mesclun
1 large cucumber, peeled, seeded, and diced

1. To make the dressing: In a small bowl, whisk together the vinegar, dill, salt, and pepper. Add the oil and whisk to combine.

2. In a large bowl, mix together the lettuce and the cucumber. Toss with the dressing before serving.

Saucy Tilapia with Tomatoes and Capers

We never get tired of the sweet, mild flavor of tilapia, but some nights we like to pair it with a nice bold sauce like this Italian combo, which offers salty capers and tangy tomatoes. Serve it with a side of rice to soak up all that delicious sauce.

SERVES 4

2 tablespoons olive oil

1 medium onion, chopped

2 garlic cloves, chopped

One 14½-ounce can diced tomatoes

3 tablespoons capers, rinsed and drained

Salt and freshly ground black pepper to taste

Four 6-ounce tilapia fillets

2 tablespoons chopped fresh basil, for garnish (optional)

1. Warm the olive oil in a large skillet over medium heat. Add the onion and cook, stirring occasionally, for 3 to 5 minutes, or until softened. Add the garlic, cook for 1 minute, then add the tomatoes, capers, salt, and pepper. Reduce the heat to medium-low and cook for 5 minutes.

2. Season the tilapia with salt and pepper. Raise the heat under the sauce to medium and simmer. Nestle the fillets in the sauce, cover, and cook for 3 minutes. Using cooking tongs or a fork, turn the fish over and continue cooking, uncovered, for 3 to 5 minutes, or until a fork goes through the thickest part of the fish with no resistance. Garnish with the basil, if desired.

Broiled Tuna with Pineapple-Chipotle Salsa

When it's so cold that even Bobby won't cook out on the grill, we turn to this recipe. Broiling tuna (one of Bobby's favorite fish) is a perfect way to sear the outside while keeping it nice and rare inside, and the superfast salsa is full of bright, spicy flavor. We started making our own salsas a few years ago and haven't looked back.

SERVES 4

SALSA

1 cup cubed pineapple, preferably fresh

¼ cup seeded and finely diced green bell pepper

3 tablespoons finely chopped scallions (white and light green parts)

1 tablespoon freshly squeezed lime juice

1 tablespoon olive oil

½ teaspoon salt

½ teaspoon seeded and minced chipotle chile in adobo sauce, or Tabasco or other hot sauce

TUNA

Four 8-ounce tuna steaks

2 tablespoons olive oil

Salt and freshly ground black pepper to taste

1. Preheat the broiler or prepare a medium-hot grill. If using the broiler, line a rimmed baking sheet with aluminum foil.

2. To make the salsa: In a small bowl, mix together the pineapple, bell pepper, scallions, lime juice, olive oil, salt, and chipotle chile. Let stand, covered, at room temperature while you prepare the tuna.

3. To make the tuna: Coat the tuna with the olive oil and season with salt and pepper. Place the tuna on the prepared baking sheet or, if grilling, place it on the grill. Broil, 4 inches from the heat, or grill for 3 minutes per side, or until the tuna is cooked to desired doneness. Serve topped with the salsa.

Seared Red Snapper with Zesty Basil Butter

Red snapper just about jump into your boat off the coast of Savannah, where there's a fishing area near us known as the snapper bank. We like to sear the fillets and serve them with a delicious sauce of lemony butter with basil. In fact, we'd probably eat anything we put this butter sauce on.

SERVES 4

3 tablespoons unsalted butter

1½ teaspoons freshly squeezed lemon juice

1 large garlic clove, finely chopped

¼ teaspoon salt, plus additional for seasoning

¼ teaspoon freshly ground black pepper, plus additional for seasoning

Four 6- to 8-ounce red snapper fillets

3 tablespoons olive oil

2 tablespoons chopped fresh basil

1. To make the butter sauce: combine the butter, lemon juice, garlic, the ¼ teaspoon salt, and ¼ teaspoon pepper in a medium saucepan and cook over low heat, stirring, until the butter melts. Cover and keep warm over low heat.

2. Score the skin side of the snapper with 3 or 4 shallow diagonal cuts. Season lightly with the additional salt and pepper. Heat the olive oil in a large skillet over medium heat. Cook the snapper skin side down for 3 minutes. Turn and cook for 3 to 4 minutes more, or until the snapper is just opaque.

3. Transfer the snapper to individual plates. Stir the basil into the melted butter mixture and spoon over the snapper to serve.

a bit more, y'all

We're serious. We would probably eat anything you spread this butter sauce on. We especially love it drizzled on mashed potatoes, toasted French bread, steamed broccoli florets, grilled chicken breasts, and pork chops. *Mmmmm.*

Couscous with Mushrooms

As soon as we discovered how fast couscous is to make—we're talking five minutes—there was no holding us back. We serve it with everything from Balsamic-Glazed London Broil (page 15) to Peppery Turkey Scaloppini (page 46).

SERVES 6

3 tablespoons olive oil
10 ounces mushrooms, quartered and thinly
   sliced
1 medium Vidalia onion, finely chopped
1½ cups chicken broth
¾ teaspoon salt
1 cup uncooked couscous
1 tablespoon chopped fresh basil, for garnish
   (optional)

1. Heat the olive oil in a medium saucepan over medium-high heat. Add the mushrooms and cook, stirring occasionally, for about 7 minutes, or until softened. Add the onion and cook for 5 minutes more.

2. Add the chicken broth and salt and bring to a boil. Stir in the couscous. Immediately remove the pan from the heat, cover it, and let stand until all the liquid is absorbed, 5 to 10 minutes.

3. Uncover and fluff the couscous with a fork. Garnish with the basil, if desired, and serve immediately.

"Nothing satisfies me more than eating a fish that's been freshly caught . . . especially when it's me that did the catching!"
— Uncle Bubba

Baked Trout with Lemon and Rosemary

PHOTOGRAPH ON PAGE 50

This recipe was born in the Smoky Mountains of Tennessee where, as kids, we went camping with our parents. We caught fresh trout, and Mama cooked them right up on the grill in foil packs. It was the best-tasting fish we'd ever had. If we're making this over a campfire, we serve it on its own. At home, it goes well with green beans.

SERVES 4

Four 12-ounce boned whole trout

Salt and freshly ground black pepper to taste

4 tablespoons unsalted butter (½ stick), cut into 16 pieces

4 fresh rosemary branches

2 lemons, each cut crosswise into 8 slices

1. Preheat the oven to 400°F.

2. Lay a 20-inch sheet of aluminum foil on a counter and place an open trout, skin side down, in the center. Season the trout with salt and pepper. Dot one side of the trout with 2 pieces of butter and top with 1 rosemary branch and 4 slices of lemon. Top the lemon with 2 more pieces of butter. Fold the other side of the trout over the filling. Fold the edges of the foil up into a tent, tuck the ends under, and press down the edges to seal. Repeat with the remaining trout.

3. Place the tents on a baking sheet and bake for 20 minutes. Transfer the tents to four plates and open carefully.

Green Beans with Black Olives

You'll be amazed at how much two ingredients can transform green beans. Blending olives with olive oil creates a chunky sauce with enough flavor to carry the day. We also love this with Italian-Style Pork Chops (page 23) and Braised Chicken with Peppers and Mushrooms (page 129).

SERVES 4

¼ cup pitted kalamata olives
2 tablespoons olive oil
½ pound green beans, trimmed

1. Combine the olives and olive oil in a blender or mini food processor and pulse to a coarse consistency.

2. Meanwhile, bring a pot of salted water to a boil. Cook the green beans until tender, 8 to 10 minutes. Drain the beans and toss with the olive mixture.

Not-Your-Mama's Tuna Casserole

Mama's spaghetti and tuna casserole was delicious. We don't want to give anyone the idea that it wasn't by calling this Not-Your-Mama's. But this casserole, full of creamed corn, olives, and cheese and topped with addictively crunchy fried onions, is really better than it has any right to be. Sorry, Mama!

SERVES 4 TO 6

6 ounces egg noodles

One 14¾-ounce can creamed corn

½ cup cream cheese (4 ounces)

½ cup milk

1 teaspoon Dijon mustard

One 6-ounce can tuna, packed in water

½ cup chopped pimiento-stuffed green olives

Salt and freshly ground black pepper to taste

1¾ cups French-fried onions

1. Preheat the oven to 375°F. Lightly grease a 9 x 13-inch baking dish.

2. Bring a large pot of salted water to a boil. Cook the egg noodles according to the package directions.

3. Meanwhile, combine the creamed corn, cream cheese, milk, and mustard in a large saucepan over medium heat. Cook, stirring occasionally, until the cream cheese melts, 3 to 5 minutes.

4. Drain the egg noodles and add to the corn mixture. Add the tuna, olives, salt, and pepper.

5. Transfer the tuna mixture to the prepared baking dish and top with the fried onions. Bake for 20 minutes, or until bubbly. Serve immediately.

SHRIMP, *Savannah Style*

We love living in Savannah for loads of reasons, but its abundance of delicious shrimp would have to be at the top of our list. Shrimping is big business here on the coast (the Gulf states provide most of the shrimp sold in America), and naturally, we cook with these tasty crustaceans every chance we get. Shrimp are so versatile that they can work into just about any recipe you've got, whether you're featuring them as the star of the meal or just grilling a handful and tossing them into a salad. Kids love them, even those kids who won't eat any other kind of fish, and fixing a simple shrimp cocktail or some fried shrimp is a great way to entice the little ones into enjoying the bounty of the sea.

If you don't live in an area with an inexpensive shrimp supply, we recommend buying bags of frozen large shrimp or buying fresh shrimp when they're on sale (shrimp season runs from May to October, and you can find them at lower prices at this time) and freezing them for use later on. In the supermarket, frozen shrimp are usually sold cleaned and ready to cook, but when you're buying fresh, it'll save you a little money if you buy them with their shells on. When you get them home, it's just a matter of peeling off the shell and using a sharp knife to remove the black vein that runs along the body of the shrimp. Cut off the tail if you'll be mixing the shrimp into something else (like pasta or salad greens); leave the tail on if the shrimp are destined for the grill or will be dipped in cocktail sauce. Rinse them under cold water, pat them dry, and you're all set.

Once you have the shrimp in hand, you'll be amazed at how quick they are to prepare. The main thing to remember is not to overcook them. Whether grilling, frying, or boiling, you'll want to take the shrimp off the heat at just the moment when they change from translucent to pink. That means you can be enjoying a yummy shrimp dinner in five minutes flat! Now, how's that for takin' it easy?

Jerk Shrimp Kebabs with Tomatoes, Onions, and Peppers

We're always looking for new ways to cook shrimp. Here, the lip-smacking shrimp and veggies cook on skewers at the same time, making the meal fast and easy enough for a weeknight meal, even if shrimp seem like Saturday-night kind of food. Kids can even help out with threading the food onto the skewers. Serve this spicy recipe over Coconut-Orange Cashew Rice (page 66) and you've got a complete and extra special meal.

SERVES 6

½ cup bottled jerk sauce

½ cup plus 2 tablespoons olive oil

1½ teaspoons peeled and finely chopped fresh ginger

Salt and freshly ground black pepper to taste

1 pound large shrimp, peeled and deveined

1 cup grape or cherry tomatoes

1 large onion, cut into chunks

1 red bell pepper, seeded and cut into ¼-inch strips

1 tablespoon chopped fresh parsley, for garnish

1. If using bamboo skewers, soak them in water for at least 20 minutes. Preheat the broiler or prepare the grill.

2. To make the marinade: In a large bowl, whisk together the jerk sauce, ½ cup of the olive oil, the ginger, salt, and pepper. Add the shrimp and toss to coat. Cover and marinate for 15 minutes.

3. In a separate bowl, toss the tomatoes and onion with the remaining 2 tablespoons olive oil. Season with salt and pepper.

4. Spread the vegetables out on a large plate and microwave them for 2 minutes. Let the vegetables cool slightly, then thread them onto skewers along with the shrimp.

5. Place the skewers on a rimmed baking sheet lined with aluminum foil, or, if grilling, place on the grill. Cook, turning once, for 5 to 6 minutes more, or until the vegetables are tender and the shrimp are opaque. Garnish with the parsley before serving.

a bit more, y'all

If you can't find jerk sauce, you can skip it and make this even simpler. Just brush the shrimp and veggies with olive oil, season with salt and pepper, and grill as directed. The shrimp won't be spicy, but their sweet flavor will really shine.

Coconut-Orange Cashew Rice

We've had some incredible West Indian food on some of the cruises we've taken, and this is our nod to those island flavors. Adventurous kids will like this slightly sweet, creamy, nutty rice. You should also try it with Broiled Tuna with Pineapple-Chipotle Salsa (page 57) and Spicy Honey Chicken Salad over Spinach (page 150).

SERVES 6

1 tablespoon olive oil
1½ cups uncooked long-grain rice
One 14-ounce can coconut milk
⅓ cup freshly squeezed orange juice
1 teaspoon salt
1 seedless orange
¾ cup chopped salted roasted cashews

1. Heat the olive oil in a large saucepan over medium-high heat. Add the rice and stir to coat with the oil. Add the coconut milk, orange juice, ⅓ cup of water, and salt and bring to a boil. Cover and reduce the heat to low. Simmer for about 20 minutes, or until all the liquid is absorbed.

2. Remove the rice from the heat and fluff with a fork. Place a clean, dry dish towel over the pan, cover with a lid, and let the rice steam for 5 minutes.

3. Cut off the top and bottom of the orange, just exposing the flesh. With a sharp knife, follow the curve of the fruit to cut away the peel, completely removing the white pith. Slice out each segment of orange, cutting along the membranes. Cut each segment into thirds. Stir the orange pieces and cashews into the rice. Serve hot.

Sautéed Shrimp with Bacon and Mushrooms

Mama likes to serve peppered shrimp in their jackets, and we've been improvising on her recipe for years. But for simple weeknight meals, we like to buy shelled shrimp. They're easier to eat that way, and faster to cook. Here, we sauté them with mushrooms, which Bobby is fond of, and bacon (you can guess who thought of adding that!).

SERVES 4

5 slices bacon (about 5 ounces), diced

10 ounces mushrooms, sliced

1 green bell pepper, seeded and diced

¼ cup sliced scallions (white and light green parts)

1 pound large shrimp, peeled and deveined

½ teaspoon salt

¾ teaspoon freshly ground black pepper

Tabasco or other hot sauce to taste

1. Brown the bacon in a large skillet over medium-high heat. Cook for 5 to 7 minutes, or until crisp. Increase the heat to high. Add the mushrooms, bell pepper, and scallions and cook for 7 to 10 minutes, or until the vegetables are softened and the mushroom liquid has mostly evaporated. Move the bacon and vegetables to one side of the skillet.

2. Add the shrimp to the skillet and cook for 3 minutes, or until just opaque. Stir all the ingredients to combine. Season with salt, pepper, and Tabasco sauce. Serve hot.

Vidalia-Onion-Stuffed Baked Potatoes with "The Deens' List" of Toppings

Some dishes are all about the garnishes. Or maybe some families like to do it up. Either way, when we bake a potato, we don't settle for a pat of butter. The fixin's are the fun part! We've made up a whole list of optional baked potato toppings, but, for us, the Vidalia onions are nonnegotiable. These crunchy and sweet onions are a Southern favorite and, although they're grown only in Georgia, they're still available in many supermarkets nationwide. If you can't get Vidalias, other sweet onions like Walla Wallas or Texas sweets taste just as good.

These taters go great with all kind of mains. Two of our other favorites are All-Day Beef Chili (page 122) and Southern-Style Turkey, Tomato, and Monterey Jack Bake (page 48).

SERVES 4 TO 6

3 large russet potatoes, scrubbed and pricked all over with a fork
3 tablespoons olive oil
1 tablespoon salt
¾ cup chopped Vidalia onion
3 tablespoons unsalted butter, cut into small pieces
3 tablespoons mayonnaise

1. Preheat the oven to 450°F.

2. Rub the potatoes with the olive oil and salt. Place the potatoes on a baking sheet and bake for 1 hour, or until tender.

3. Allow the potatoes to cool slightly and, when just cool enough to handle, slice them in half lengthwise.

4. Divide the chopped onion, butter, and mayonnaise over the cut sides of the potatoes and, using a fork, mash them into the potatoes. Serve hot, providing small bowls of The Deens' List of Toppings (below), if desired, so everyone can customize his or her own potato.

THE DEENS' LIST OF TOPPINGS

Sour cream
Chopped fresh chives
Cooked, crumbled bacon
Shredded cheddar cheese
Chopped pitted kalamata olives

a bit more, y'all

When you (or your kids) are hungry, an hour can seem like a lifetime to wait for that potato to bake. We usually throw a few spuds into the oven when we're doing the Sunday roast. When the potatoes are done, we just wrap them in aluminum foil and keep them in the fridge. Then, they're all ready to be reheated and stuffed for the next night's dinner.

Spicy Oven-Baked Pepper Shrimp

This is another quick-and-easy way to prepare shrimp that are smooth and buttery, with just the right amount of peppery fire to keep your family on its toes. We usually serve these with baked potatoes and a little bit of green salad on the side. Just pop the shrimp in the oven when the spuds are almost done and bring it all out to the table piping hot.

SERVES 4 TO 6

4 tablespoons (½ stick) unsalted butter

4 tablespoons olive oil

2 garlic cloves, minced

1 tablespoon freshly ground black pepper

1 teaspoon salt

½ teaspoon crushed red pepper flakes

2 pounds large shrimp, peeled and deveined

4 scallions (white and light green parts), thinly sliced, for garnish

1. Preheat the oven to 450°F.

2. Combine the butter, olive oil, garlic, black pepper, salt, and red pepper flakes in a small casserole dish. Bake until the butter is melted and bubbling, 3 to 5 minutes.

3. Add the shrimp to the butter mixture, stirring to combine. Bake for 5 minutes.

4. Stir the mixture once more and bake until the shrimp are just opaque, 3 to 5 minutes more. Garnish with the scallions and serve hot.

"I might grab a Diet Coke and call it breakfast, but I sit down every night for dinner, knowing it'll probably be the highlight of my day." —Jamie

Shrimp 'n' Grits

This dish is a true Southern delight, our riff on Louisiana-style spicy shrimp combined with cheesy grits just the way we make 'em at The Lady & Sons. It's amazing how easy this is to whip up. Make it for your family, and they'll swear you spent all day tied to the stove.

SERVES 4 TO 6

GRITS

3 cups milk

½ teaspoon salt

1½ cups old-fashioned grits

3 cups grated cheddar cheese (12 ounces)

SHRIMP

6 tablespoons unsalted butter

6 tablespoons all-purpose flour

2 medium green bell peppers, seeded and chopped

2 medium onions, chopped

2 jalapeño peppers, seeded and finely chopped

2 garlic cloves, minced

1½ teaspoons salt

Freshly ground black pepper to taste

2 cups heavy cream

Two 14½-ounce cans diced tomatoes

2 pounds large shrimp, peeled and deveined

Tabasco or other hot sauce to taste

½ cup grated Parmesan cheese, for garnish

2 tablespoons chopped fresh parsley, for garnish

1. To make the grits: Combine 4 cups of water, the milk, and salt in a large saucepan over medium-high heat. Bring the mixture to a boil and slowly whisk in the grits. Reduce the heat to medium-low. Cover the saucepan and simmer, stirring occasionally, for about 15 minutes, or until thickened. Stir in the cheddar cheese. Cover and keep warm over a low heat.

2. To make the shrimp: Melt the butter in a large skillet over medium heat. Add the flour and cook, stirring, until the mixture is dark and golden, about 5 minutes. Add the bell peppers, onions, jalapeños, garlic, ½ teaspoon of the salt, and pepper. Cook until the vegetables are softened, about 5 minutes.

3. Slowly whisk in the cream. Once the cream is fully incorporated, slowly whisk in the tomatoes and ⅔ cup of water. Stir in the shrimp and cook, stirring occasionally, until the shrimp are just opaque, about 5 minutes.

4. Season the shrimp with the remaining 1 teaspoon salt, pepper, and Tabasco. Serve the shrimp over the grits and garnish with the Parmesan cheese and parsley.

Butter-Braised Shrimp

A lemony butter sauce infuses these shrimp with a flavor that is perky and decadent all at once. You'll be tempted to serve it over all your seafood dishes. But look out! You may find yourself talking in a Georgia drawl by the end of the meal. Serve this dish with white rice or Easy Almond Rice Pilaf (page 47) for a no-fuss fancy meal.

SERVES 4 TO 6

8 tablespoons (1 stick) unsalted butter

6 tablespoons freshly squeezed lemon juice

1 teaspoon salt

Freshly ground black pepper to taste

2 pounds large shrimp, peeled and deveined

1. Combine the butter, lemon juice, salt, and pepper in a large skillet over medium heat. Cook the mixture, stirring constantly, for about 1 minute, or until the butter melts.

2. Stir in the shrimp. Cover the pan and reduce the heat to medium-low. Cook, stirring occasionally, for about 5 minutes, or until the shrimp are just opaque.

grilling

Grilled food is always delicious. The high heat seals in moisture and flavor, and you get that brown, crisp, caramelized exterior that makes you hungry just thinking about it. Probably the biggest reason we love grilling as much as we do is that we're always spending time outside. Down South, there is so much perfect weather that grilling never feels like work, especially when we're out hanging around with friends. Plus, early evening is a great time of day to let the kids go wild outdoors. While we're flipping burgers, Jack runs off the last of his energy playing with Champ, our loyal bulldog, in the backyard.

We grill just about everything, from meat to chicken to fish to vegetables. If you've got a gas grill, you've got push-button heat that makes tasty fire-blackened dishes almost instantly, and if you're cooking over coals (we do both), you get that extra smoky flavor in there. All you need is a grill in your yard and decent weather, and you've got yourself an evening plan to look forward to at the end of a hard day. As a bonus, there are no dirty pots and pans. For that reason alone, Bobby will create entire menus that he can cook out back.

Whether you're firing up the grill for **Grilled Sausage, Pepper, and Onion Subs** (page 84) or for our **Fabulous Grilled Burgers** (page 78), if your friends live anywhere in the vicinity (or if you've busted out the portable grill to tailgate a University of Georgia home game— Go, Dawgs!), you may want to plan to make extra. There's something about the smell of barbecue on the wind that just draws folks to the grill like moths to the flame. Even when Bobby is on his own, he always makes a little more—and not just because he loves leftovers. Friends just seem to pop over when they smell barbecue—and we can't blame them.

Jamie and Bobby's Fabulous Grilled Burgers with "The Deens' List" of Toppings

When it comes to burgers, we Deens mean business. We like to keep the seasonings on the meat simple, then go all out on the toppings. Mama got us started with a fried egg on top of the burger, which can get messy, but then again, by the time we finish piling it all on—bacon, avocado, lettuce, tomato, grilled mushrooms and onions, pickles, steak sauce—well, it's a three-napkin burger at the very least.

SERVES 6

1¼ pounds ground beef

2 teaspoons Worcestershire sauce

1½ teaspoons salt

1 teaspoon freshly ground black pepper

6 toasted hamburger buns, for serving

1. Prepare a medium grill.

2. In a bowl, mix together the beef, Worcestershire sauce, salt, and pepper. Use your hands to form the mixture into 6 equal-size patties.

3. Grill the burgers, flipping once, to desired doneness, 12 minutes for medium-rare, up to 14 minutes for medium. Serve on toasted buns and pile on the toppings.

THE DEENS' LIST OF TOPPINGS

Fried egg	Mustard
Shredded iceberg lettuce	Mayonnaise
Sliced beefsteak tomatoes	Cheddar cheese
Sliced avocado	Bacon
Thinly sliced raw onions	Grilled portobello mushroom caps
Sliced grilled onions	Sweet pickle slices
Ketchup	Steak sauce

Cheaters' Grilled "Fries" with Cajun Seasonings

If you've ever baked frozen fries inside while you were flipping your burgers outside on the grill, you might have wished you could just grill your fries, too. Well, we got sick of wishing and gave it a shot. These get nice and crisp, and we toss them with a little spice to make them that much more special.

SERVES 4

One 2-pound bag frozen French fries
Cajun seasoning to taste
Salt to taste

1. Prepare a medium-high grill.
2. Working in two batches, if necessary, place the fries in a grill basket (see A Bit More, Y'all, page 88). Grill for 15 to 20 minutes, or until the fries are crispy and golden. Season with the Cajun seasoning and salt. Serve hot.

a bit more, y'all

You can fry your eggs in any skillet if you have a side burner on your gas grill. Alternatively, heat a cast-iron skillet right on the grill, add oil, and crack in the eggs just as the burgers are finishing up.

"Grilling outside turns cooking time into playtime." —Jamie

The Ultimate Spice-Rubbed Rib Steak

A nice, thick bone-in steak, especially one served with Grilled Bacon and Cheese Jalapeño Poppers (page 82) and Vidalia-Onion–Stuffed Baked Potatoes (page 68), is our favorite kind of splurge. Uncle Bubba loves to gnaw on a steak bone, so we came up with this simple recipe for steak rubbed with brown sugar and spices especially for him. Rib eye is Bubba's favorite cut, but you can use this rub on your favorite cut, too. It's also great on grilled chicken.

SERVES 2 TO 4

2 teaspoons packed light brown sugar

2 teaspoons The Lady's House Seasoning (page 7)

½ teaspoon Cajun seasoning

¼ teaspoon cayenne pepper or to taste

Two 1-pound bone-in rib-eye steaks

1. Prepare a medium grill or preheat the broiler. If using the broiler, line a rimmed baking sheet with aluminum foil.

2. In a small bowl, combine the brown sugar, house seasoning, Cajun seasoning, and cayenne pepper. Rub the steaks with the mixture.

3. Place the steaks on the grill or, if broiling, place on the prepared baking sheet. Grill or broil, 4 inches from the heat, turning once, to desired doneness, 12 minutes for medium-rare, up to 14 minutes for medium.

"Grilling steak has a major bonus: waking up the next morning and making steak and eggs, baby!"
—Bobby

Grilled Bacon and Cheese Jalapeño Poppers

Cheese, peppers, bacon, grill . . . This is a winning combo that will steal the fire from anything else you have going on. Well, except maybe the Super Bowl, which it will make just that much better. Serve it anytime you've got a group of buddies coming over, which, for Bobby, is nearly every night. We love these with our ultimate rib steak and also with All-Day Beef Chili (page 122).

SERVES 4

½ cup grated Monterey Jack cheese (2 ounces)
¼ cup chopped fresh cilantro
8 large jalapeño peppers
8 strips bacon (about 8 ounces)

1. Prepare a medium-hot grill or preheat the broiler. If using the broiler, line a rimmed baking sheet with aluminum foil. Soak 16 wooden toothpicks for at least ½ hour.

2. In a small bowl, mix together the Monterey Jack cheese and cilantro.

3. Using a paring knife, cut the top off the peppers and reserve. Scoop out the veins and the seeds, discarding both. Stuff the cheese mixture inside the peppers, packing it tightly. Replace the cap on each pepper.

4. Using a toothpick or skewer (depending on the size of your jalapeño), skewer the peppers lengthwise from the bottom through the cap. Wrap a slice of bacon top to bottom around each pepper, covering the cap, and secure with a toothpick. Place the peppers on the grill or, if broiling, place on the prepared baking sheet. Grill or broil, turning occasionally, for 20 minutes total, or until the bacon is crisp and the peppers are tender.

"Nothing goes better with a cold beer than a hot pepper—unless it's a hot pepper wrapped in bacon!"—Uncle Bubba

Grilled Sausage, Pepper, and Onion Sub Sandwich

We first wrapped our faces around some authentic cheesesteaks and hoagies when we were shooting an episode of our Food Network show, *Road Tasted*, at Campo's Deli in Philadelphia. Once we got a taste for Yankee-style sub sandwiches, there was no going back. Grilled onions, peppers, and meat plus melted cheese all piled onto a nice big roll—you can't improve on that! Now you don't need to be in Philly to savor this supreme sandwich experience.

SERVES 8

1 green bell pepper, seeded and cut into ½-inch-thick strips

1 Vidalia or white onion, cut into ½-inch-thick strips

2 tablespoons olive oil

The Lady's House Seasoning (page 7) to taste

1 pound (about 4 sausages) sweet Italian sausages, pierced in several places with a fork

4 hoagie rolls, halved lengthwise

2 tablespoons unsalted butter

1 cup shredded mozzarella (4 ounces)

1. Prepare a medium grill or preheat the broiler. If using the broiler, line two rimmed baking sheets with aluminum foil.

2. In a bowl, combine the bell pepper, onion, olive oil, and house seasoning and toss well to combine.

3. Place the sausages on the grill or, if broiling, place on one of the prepared baking sheets. Grill or broil, 4 inches from the heat, turning occasionally, for 20 to 25 minutes total, or until the sausages are cooked through and no longer pink.

4. Place the pepper and onion strips in a grilling basket (see A Bit More, Y'all, page 88) or, if broiling, place on the second prepared baking sheet. Grill or broil, turning occasionally, for 20 to 25 minutes total, or until the vegetables are tender.

5. Spread the cut sides of the rolls with the butter and grill or broil cut side down for about 2 minutes. Slice the sausages in half lengthwise and divide the halves among the bottom halves of the rolls. Divide the vegetables equally among the rolls and sprinkle equal amounts of mozzarella on each. Cover with the top halves of the rolls and wrap tightly in aluminum foil. Grill or broil for 3 to 4 minutes, or until the mozzarella is melted.

Bobby's Special Thick-Cut Garlic Pork Chops with Bourbon Glaze

PHOTOGRAPH ON PAGE 74

When Bobby caught on to thick-cut pork chops, they started disappearing from the walk-in refrigerator at The Lady & Sons. We both enjoy how juicy and satisfying a nice big chop is, especially since it's not as heavy as red meat and not as easy to dry out as a thinner chop. This is a simple, tasty way to cook them. All you need to add is some grilled veggies to make a complete meal.

SERVES 2 TO 4

2 tablespoons Dijon mustard

1 tablespoon packed dark brown sugar

1 tablespoon Bourbon

Two ¾- to 1-pound (1¼ to 1½ inches thick) center-cut, bone-in pork chops

1 garlic clove, halved

The Lady's House Seasoning (page 7) to taste

1. Prepare a medium-hot grill or preheat the broiler. If using the broiler, line a rimmed baking sheet with aluminum foil.

2. To make the glaze: In a bowl, mix together the mustard, brown sugar, and Bourbon. Rub the pork chops with the garlic and house seasoning, then brush with half the glaze.

3. Place the chops on the grill or, if broiling, place on the prepared baking sheet. Grill or broil, 4 inches from the heat, turning once, until the chops are slightly charred and cooked through (a hint of pink will remain in the center), 20 minutes total. Brush with the remaining glaze before serving.

Good-for-You Grilled Vegetable Basket

If you've already got the grill going, this is a surefire way to get great veggies fast. They get deliciously smoky-sweet, and all you need is a handy grill basket to keep the small pieces from falling into the fire (or you can use a sheet of aluminum foil). A colorful assortment of veggies makes this especially fun. You can serve it with any of the grilling recipes in the chapter, but it's especially great with Grilled Tilapia Po'boys with Homemade Tartar Sauce (page 95) and Easy After-Work BBQ Chicken (page 91).

SERVES 4

8 ounces cremini mushrooms

1 zucchini, cut into ¼-inch-thick slices

1 red bell pepper, seeded and cut into ¼-inch-thick slices

1 Vidalia or white onion, cut into ¼-inch-thick rings

⅓ cup bottled balsamic vinegar salad dressing

1. Prepare the grill or preheat the broiler. If using the broiler, line a rimmed baking sheet with aluminum foil.

2. Combine the mushrooms, zucchini, bell pepper, onion, and salad dressing in a shallow dish and allow the vegetables to marinate while the grill or broiler heats up.

3. Place the vegetables in a grilling basket or, if broiling, place on the prepared baking sheet. Grill or broil, 4 inches from the heat, turning once, until the vegetables are slightly charred and cooked through, 20 minutes total.

a bit more, y'all

Grilling baskets are available at most housewares stores. Or you can place a sheet of aluminum foil over the grill grate to prevent small or messy ingredients, such as vegetables or fish, from falling into the fire.

Grilled Caesar Pork Tenderloin

You can order yourself a grilled chicken Caesar anywhere. But we figured we could jazz up that combo a little while still keeping it fairly healthful if we swapped in tender slices of grilled pork instead. The smoky, juicy pork and crunchy, tangy salad is a uniquely delicious pairing, if we do say so ourselves. We love to serve it with our Grilled Cheesy Olive Bread (page 90), but then again, we love just about anything with that bread!

SERVES 4

Two 1-pound pork tenderloins

1 cup bottled Caesar salad dressing

Two 10-ounce bags (about 16 cups total) romaine lettuce

2 cups garlic-flavored croutons

½ cup coarsely grated Parmesan cheese (2 ounces)

½ teaspoon freshly ground black pepper

1. Prepare a medium-hot grill or preheat the broiler. If using the broiler, line a rimmed baking sheet with aluminum foil.

2. While the grill or broiler is heating up, place the pork and ½ cup of the Caesar dressing in a shallow dish and turn to coat. Let marinate for 20 minutes, or until the grill or broiler is ready.

3. Place the pork on the grill or, if broiling, place on the prepared baking sheet. Grill or broil, 4 inches from the heat, basting with the marinade after 5 minutes. Cook, turning once, for about 20 minutes total, or until an instant-read thermometer inserted in the thickest part of the meat registers 150°F. Transfer the pork to a cutting board and cover loosely with aluminum foil. Discard any remaining marinade.

4. In a large bowl, toss together the lettuce, croutons, Parmesan cheese, pepper, and the remaining ½ cup Caesar dressing.

5. Divide the salad among four large shallow bowls. Cut the pork tenderloins into slices ½ inch thick and serve on top of the salad.

Grilled Cheesy Olive Bread

This is not only a fabulous side dish to add to the grill while the main meal is being prepared; we also love to serve it on its own as a game-day snack. You can also try it with Bobby's Special Thick-Cut Garlic Pork Chops with Bourbon Glaze (page 87) or Jamie and Bobby's Fabulous Grilled Burgers with "The Deens' List" of Toppings (page 78).

SERVES 6

1 cup grated pepper Jack cheese (4 ounces)
½ cup pitted green olives
2 tablespoons unsalted butter, softened
2 tablespoons cream cheese, softened
1 teaspoon garlic powder
1 loaf Italian bread, halved lengthwise

1. Prepare a medium-high grill or preheat the broiler.

2. Combine the pepper Jack cheese, olives, butter, cream cheese, and garlic powder in a food processor and pulse until smooth. Slather the cheese mixture over the cut halves of bread and sandwich the halves together.

3. Wrap the loaf in aluminum foil and place on the grill or, if broiling, under the broiler. Grill or broil, 4 inches from the heat, turning once, for 10 to 15 minutes total, or until the edges of the bread are crisp and golden and the cheese mixture is melted. Slice the bread and serve hot.

Easy After-Work BBQ Chicken

At The Lady & Sons, barbecued chicken and fried chicken are staples of our business—that's what we're known for. And barbecued chicken is the first thing on the list when we think about firing up the grill. It's a classic. We add a squeeze of lime juice and some zest to bring out the smoky sweetness of the sauce. What you really want to taste is the fire—that's our favorite flavor.

SERVES 4

One 3½-pound chicken, cut into 8 pieces

Salt and freshly ground black pepper to taste

2 cups bottled sauce or Easy BBQ Sauce (recipe follows)

3 tablespoons chopped scallions (white and light green parts)

1½ teaspoons freshly grated lime zest

1½ tablespoons freshly squeezed lime juice

Lime wedges, for serving

1. Prepare a medium-hot grill or preheat the broiler. If using the broiler, line a rimmed baking sheet with aluminum foil.

2. Season the chicken with salt and pepper. In a small bowl, combine the barbecue sauce with the scallions, lime zest, and lime juice. Reserve ½ cup of the sauce mixture for serving. Coat the chicken with half of the remaining sauce.

3. Place the chicken on the grill or, if broiling, place on the prepared baking sheet. Grill or broil, 4 inches from the heat, turning once, for 10 minutes per side. Baste with the remaining half of the sauce and grill or broil for 5 minutes more. Transfer to a serving platter, drizzle with the reserved ½ cup sauce, and serve with the lime wedges.

Easy BBQ Sauce

If there's no time to pick up a bottle of BBQ sauce in the after-work rush, here's a simple homemade recipe using ingredients you probably already have in the fridge or pantry.

MAKES 2 CUPS

¾ cup ketchup

¼ cup plus 2 tablespoons packed dark brown sugar

3 tablespoons white wine vinegar

2 tablespoons minced onion

2 tablespoons Dijon mustard

¼ to 1 teaspoon Tabasco or other hot sauce to taste

¼ teaspoon freshly ground black pepper

In a small bowl, whisk together the ketchup, brown sugar, vinegar, onion, mustard, Tabasco, and pepper. Cover and refrigerate for up to 1 week.

Grilled Chicken Breasts with Brown Sugar Pineapple Rings

We took Mama's classic pineapple rings off the ham and put them on our grilled chicken breasts. This sweet-and-sour, quick-cooking dish is a real crowd-pleaser. Pineapple slices coated in brown sugar and Bourbon turn sweet and caramelized on the grill, and a salad dressing marinade makes the chicken tangy, moist, and tender. Perfect with a nice green spinach salad.

SERVES 4

4 boneless skinless chicken breast halves

Salt and freshly ground black pepper to taste

¼ cup bottled Italian salad dressing

One 20-ounce can pineapple slices, drained

1 tablespoon packed dark brown sugar

2 tablespoons Bourbon

1. Prepare a medium-hot grill or preheat the broiler. If using the broiler, line two rimmed baking sheets with aluminum foil.

2. While the grill or broiler is heating up, season the chicken breasts with salt and pepper and coat with the Italian dressing.

3. In a bowl, toss the pineapple slices with the brown sugar, Bourbon, and a pinch of salt.

4. Place the chicken on the grill or, if broiling, place on one of the prepared baking sheets. Grill or broil, 4 inches from the heat, turning once, for 16 to 20 minutes total, or until the chicken is slightly charred and the juices run clear when it is pricked with a fork.

5. Place the pineapple on the grill or, if broiling, place on the second prepared baking sheet. Grill or broil, turning once, for 8 to 10 minutes total, or until the pineapple is slightly charred and the sugar has caramelized. Serve the chicken with the pineapple on the side.

Spinach Salad with Dried Cranberries and Almonds

This is Brooke's favorite kind of salad—nutty and sweet (just like her dear husband maybe?). It's a light, tasty side that goes with just about anything, but especially with a rich dish, like Sautéed Ravioli with Cheese and Bread Crumbs (page 166) or Buttery Chicken "Scampi" Pasta (page 106).

SERVES 4

3 tablespoons olive oil
1 tablespoon freshly squeezed lemon juice
½ teaspoon salt
Freshly ground black pepper to taste
One 5-ounce bag (about 8 cups) baby spinach
½ cup dried cranberries
½ cup chopped roasted salted almonds

1. To make the dressing: In a small bowl, whisk together the olive oil, lemon juice, salt, and pepper.

2. In a separate bowl, combine the spinach, dried cranberries, and almonds. Pour the dressing over the salad and toss to combine.

Grilled Tilapia Po'boys with Homemade Tartar Sauce

Trust a riverboat captain to throw some fish on the grill. Mama's husband, Michael Groover, makes his po'boy sandwiches with sweet, mild tilapia fillets and tartar sauce so tasty some of us have been known to eat it on its own. These po'boys are a big, messy, and delicious meal—a real Low Country favorite. Don't forget to put a bottle of Tabasco on the table for extra punch!

SERVES 4

½ cup mayonnaise

2 tablespoons chopped sweet pickles

2 tablespoons chopped red onion

1½ teaspoons freshly squeezed lemon juice

¼ teaspoon garlic powder

Four 7-ounce tilapia fillets

Olive oil, for brushing

¼ teaspoon salt

¼ teaspoon freshly ground black pepper

1 or 2 loaves French bread (enough for four 7-inch sandwiches)

2 medium beefsteak tomatoes, cut into 8 slices total

4 romaine lettuce leaves

1. Prepare a medium grill or preheat the broiler. If using the broiler, line a rimmed baking sheet with aluminum foil.

2. To make the tartar sauce: In a small bowl, combine the mayonnaise, pickles, onion, lemon juice, and garlic powder. Cover and refrigerate until ready to use.

3. Brush the tilapia fillets with the olive oil and season with the salt and pepper. Cut the bread into four 7-inch sections and cut each section in half lengthwise.

4. Place the tilapia on the grill or, if broiling, place on the prepared baking sheet. Grill or broil, 4 inches from the heat, turning once, for about 6 minutes total, or until the tilapia flakes easily with a fork and is cooked through. Lay the bread on the grill or broiler cut side down and grill or broil for about 1 minute, or until toasted.

5. For each po'boy, place 1 tilapia fillet on the bottom slice of bread, followed by 2 slices of tomato and 1 lettuce leaf. Spread the top slice of bread with 2 tablespoons of the tartar sauce and place it on top of the sandwich.

a bit more, y'all

The best way to keep fish or other items from sticking to your grill grate is to keep it clean. Brush the grate with a stiff wire brush before you light the fire.

pasta and friends

We decided to include a chapter called Jack's Favorites in this book, but this pasta chapter could have the same title. The fact of the matter is that the kid (and most kids) would be perfectly happy eating nothing but hot buttered noodles for every meal. And we can see where he's coming from. Pasta—or macaroni, as we called it growing up—has always been a food we love too much to ever get tired of.

Mama pretty much stuck with elbow macaroni, baked with cheese or tossed with mayonnaise for a salad, but as adults, we've come to appreciate how many different shapes of pasta there are, and how wonderful they can be with just about anything from seafood to vegetables to bacon. In fact, serving an ingredient tossed with pasta is one of the easiest ways to introduce a new food to kids (though Jack once spent a half hour picking cubes of Mama's delicious baked ham out of a dish of pasta and peas that we tried giving him—you know, if at first you don't succeed . . .).

For fast suppers, a box of dried pasta and a can of tomatoes in the pantry, Parmesan cheese in the fridge, and some sausage and peas in the freezer will get you one of our favorite weeknight meals: **Creamy, Spicy Sausage Pasta** (page 105). And when you've got a little more time before dinner, baked pasta is the ultimate family-pleaser: What's better than browned, bubbling cheese on top of pasta? You can put together a recipe like **Hearty Bacon and Beef Pasta Casserole** (page 103) in no time, then get your salad going and maybe put your feet up while the pasta bakes. Plus, those baked pasta casseroles are the number-one hit with kids and adults at potluck dinners. In fact, we might just as well call this chapter Everyone's Favorites!

Quick Spaghetti and Meatballs

When we think of spaghetti and meatballs, we think of someone's Italian grandma in the kitchen all day. But we love this childhood favorite too much to wait for it, so we just had to make our own, weeknight version. Add Cheesy Garlic Bread (page 102), and you just can't get a tastier meal in less time.

SERVES 4

1 pound ground beef

6 tablespoons grated Parmesan cheese, plus additional for serving

¼ cup plain unseasoned bread crumbs

1 large egg, lightly beaten

2 tablespoons The Lady's House Seasoning (page 7)

1 tablespoon dried oregano

3 tablespoons olive oil

One 24-ounce jar marinara sauce

1 pound spaghetti

1. In a bowl, combine the beef, Parmesan cheese, bread crumbs, egg, house seasoning, and oregano. Use your hands to form the mixture into 2-inch round meatballs.

2. Heat the olive oil in a large skillet over medium-high heat. Add the meatballs and cook, turning occasionally, for 5 to 10 minutes total, or until golden brown. Add the marinara sauce and reduce the heat to medium. Simmer for 15 to 20 minutes, or until the meatballs are no longer pink. Cover and keep warm.

3. Bring a large pot of salted water to a boil. Cook the spaghetti according to the package directions. Drain well. Divide the spaghetti among four shallow bowls and top with the meatballs and sauce. Garnish with Parmesan cheese.

Cheesy Garlic Bread

If time and busy schedules allowed, we'd still show up at Mama's table around 3:30 p.m. every day begging for an afternoon snack of cheese bread. Instead, we now work the bread into our dinner routine. You can even serve this on its own or with a salad for lunch. Or, try it with Braised Chicken with Peppers and Mushrooms (page 129) and Not-Your-Mama's Tuna Casserole (page 62).

SERVES 4 TO 6

1 loaf Italian bread, halved lengthwise
8 tablespoons (1 stick) unsalted butter
3 tablespoons chopped fresh parsley
2 garlic cloves, finely chopped
½ teaspoon salt
2 cups grated Monterey Jack cheese (8 ounces)

1. Preheat the oven to 350°F.
2. Melt the butter in a small saucepan over medium heat, or in a microwave. Stir in the parsley, garlic, and salt. Spoon the butter mixture over the cut sides of the bread. Scatter the cheese over the bottom half of the loaf, and top with the other half.

3. Wrap the loaf in aluminum foil and transfer to a baking sheet. Bake for 15 to 20 minutes, or until the cheese is melted. Using a serrated knife, slice the bread and serve immediately.

"What I miss most about being a kid is slurping up spaghetti so fast it whips you in the face. The messier the better!" — Bobby

Hearty Bacon and Beef Pasta Casserole

Like Mama's goulash, this easy, meaty baked spaghetti is based on ground beef. We add olives, Alfredo sauce, and bacon to give it loads of flavor. This is one of those dishes that folks line up for at a church dinner or school fund-raiser. It's not much more complicated than following the instructions on the back of the Hamburger Helper box—but it's a whole lot more satisfying. Serve it with a tasty and hearty green salad like our Crisp Romaine and Tomato Salad (page 115).

SERVES 6

1 pound spaghetti

8 strips bacon (about 8 ounces), diced

1 pound ground beef

1 medium onion, finely diced

½ cup chopped pitted green olives (optional)

Pinch of crushed red pepper flakes

Three 10-ounce containers Alfredo sauce, preferably fresh from your supermarket's refrigerator case

3 tablespoons chopped fresh parsley

½ cup grated Parmesan cheese (2 ounces)

1. Bring a large pot of salted water to a boil. Cook the spaghetti according to the package directions. Drain well and transfer to a large bowl.

2. Preheat the oven to 375°F. Grease a 9 x 13-inch baking dish.

3. Fry the bacon in a large skillet over medium-high heat until brown, about 5 minutes. Using a slotted spoon, transfer the bacon to a paper-towel-lined plate. Pour off the drippings from the skillet. Add the beef, onion, olives (if using), and red pepper flakes. Cook, breaking up the beef with a fork, for 7 to 10 minutes, or until the beef is brown and the onion is soft.

4. Remove the skillet from the heat and stir in the Alfredo sauce. Sprinkle in the parsley and bacon and stir. Pour the sauce over the spaghetti and toss to combine.

5. Transfer the pasta to the prepared baking dish and top with the Parmesan cheese. Bake until golden on top, about 30 minutes.

Creamy, Spicy Sausage Pasta

Any recipe that includes the words *creamy*, *spicy*, and *sausage* is going to get our attention. For this number we just add peas for a little sweetness and color, then serve it over rigatoni. Not only is this dish satisfying and elegant, but you can have it on the table in the time it takes to cook the pasta.

SERVES 4 TO 6

1 tablespoon olive oil

1 pound (about 4 sausages) hot or sweet Italian sausages, casings removed

¾ cup heavy cream

¾ cup prepared tomato sauce

1½ cups frozen peas, thawed

Salt and freshly ground black pepper to taste

1 pound rigatoni pasta

Grated Parmesan cheese, for garnish

1. Heat the olive oil in a large skillet over medium heat. Crumble the sausages into the pan and cook until browned, 3 to 5 minutes. Stir in the cream and tomato sauce and simmer until slightly thickened, about 5 minutes. Add the peas and cook for 2 minutes more. Season with salt and pepper.

2. Meanwhile, bring a large pot of salted water to a boil. Cook the rigatoni according to the package directions. Drain well. Add the rigatoni to the sauce in the skillet and stir to combine. Serve with grated Parmesan cheese.

a bit more, y'all

Buy your Parmesan cheese in a block and grate it right at the table, restaurant-style. Cheese that's not pregrated has a better flavor—and it's cheaper to boot!

"Something about creamy foods speaks to my heart." —Jamie

Buttery Chicken "Scampi" Pasta

Jamie's a fan of shrimp scampi, but Jack is not. Turns out they can both agree on this chicken version.

SERVES 4

4 tablespoons (½ stick) unsalted butter

2 tablespoons olive oil

4 garlic cloves, minced

¾ cup dry white wine

1¼ teaspoons salt, plus additional for seasoning

¼ teaspoon freshly ground black pepper, plus additional for seasoning

⅛ teaspoon crushed red pepper flakes

3 boneless skinless chicken breast halves, cut into 1½-inch-long strips

⅓ cup chopped fresh parsley

1½ tablespoons freshly squeezed lemon juice

Cooked pasta, such as linguine, for serving

1. Melt the butter with the olive oil in a large skillet over medium heat. Add the garlic and cook for 1 minute, until fragrant. Add the wine, the 1¼ teaspoons salt, the ¼ teaspoon pepper, and the red pepper flakes. Simmer until the wine has reduced by half, 3 to 5 minutes.

2. Season the chicken with the additional salt and pepper. Add the chicken to the sauce in the skillet and cook for 5 minutes, or until no longer pink inside and the juices run clear when it is pricked with a fork. Stir in the parsley and lemon juice. Serve over the pasta.

Spicy Southern Shrimp and Pasta Bake

If you've been to Savannah, or if you live here (hey, neighbor!), then you know that we're one shrimp-crazy city. We like shrimp so well we are happy just boiling them up and eating them out of their shells. But every once in a while, we do something a little more substantial for dinner, like this Cajun-flavored dish, which goes great with our colorful Broccoli and Red Pepper Salad (page 109).

SERVES 4 TO 6

5 tablespoons unsalted butter

1 cup finely chopped onions

¾ pound large shrimp, peeled, deveined, and cut into thirds

1 cup frozen corn kernels, thawed

1 cup frozen sliced okra, thawed

½ teaspoon salt

½ teaspoon Cajun seasoning

One 24-ounce jar tomato sauce

½ cup cream cheese (4 ounces)

1 pound corkscrew pasta, cooked and drained

⅔ cup plain unseasoned bread crumbs

1. Preheat the oven to 400°F.

2. Melt 2 tablespoons of the butter in a very large skillet over medium-high heat. Add the onions and cook for 5 minutes, or until translucent. Add the shrimp, corn, okra, salt, and Cajun seasoning. Cook, stirring, for 2 to 3 minutes, or until the shrimp are almost opaque. Add the tomato sauce and cream cheese and cook, stirring, for 3 to 4 minutes, or until the sauce is smooth.

3. Place the pasta in a 9 x 13-inch baking dish. Pour the shrimp mixture over the pasta and stir well.

4. Return the skillet to the heat and melt the remaining 3 tablespoons butter. Add the bread crumbs and stir until well coated.

5. Top the casserole with the bread crumbs and bake for 15 to 20 minutes, or until golden brown. Serve immediately.

Broccoli and Red Bell Pepper Salad

Bobby loves broccoli; Jamie loves bacon; Brooke loves pine nuts and dried cranberries; and everybody loves ranch dressing, so this salad just kind of "appeared" in the bowl one day when we were all feeling hungry. Also try it with Quick-'n'-Easy Chicken 'n' Dumplings (page 131).

SERVES 4

5 strips bacon (about 5 ounces)
1 pound broccoli, cut into florets
1 cup seeded and cubed red bell pepper
½ cup grated cheddar cheese (2 ounces)
⅓ cup pine nuts, toasted
¼ cup dried cranberries
½ cup bottled ranch salad dressing

1. Cook the bacon in a skillet over medium-high heat for 5 to 7 minutes, or until crisp. Transfer to a paper-towel-lined plate to drain.

2. In a large bowl, combine the broccoli, bell pepper, cheddar cheese, pine nuts, and dried cranberries. Crumble in the bacon and pour in the dressing. Toss well to combine. Let sit for 20 minutes before serving.

"If you've got pasta in your pantry, you've got dinner halfway made."
— Jamie

Savannah Baked Bow Ties and Black-eyed Peas

PHOTOGRAPH ON PAGE 96

One of our favorite things about pasta is that you can get creative with your sauce. Bell peppers, black-eyed peas, and Tabasco give this baked pasta a racy Southern taste. Jamie and his family eat so much pasta at their house that we like to joke that if they weren't from the South, they'd be from southern Italy.

SERVES 4 TO 6

8 tablespoons (1 stick) unsalted butter

6 scallions (white and light green parts), chopped

1 green bell pepper, seeded and diced

3 large beefsteak tomatoes, chopped

One 15-ounce can black-eyed peas, rinsed and drained

2½ teaspoons Tabasco or other hot sauce

2¼ teaspoons salt

1 pound bow tie pasta, cooked and drained

1¼ cups grated Parmesan cheese (5 ounces)

1. Preheat the oven to 400°F.

2. Melt the butter in a large skillet over medium-high heat. Add the scallions and bell pepper and cook for 5 minutes. Stir in the tomatoes, black-eyed peas, Tabasco, and salt. Cook for 5 minutes more, until some of the juice has evaporated. Add the bow ties and toss to combine.

3. Transfer the mixture to a 9 x 13-inch baking dish and top with the Parmesan cheese. Bake for 20 minutes, or until the cheese is melted and bubbly.

Stewed Collard Greens

Some traditional Southern cooks swear you have to cook your collards all day long. This recipe has a great silky, tender texture and good bacony flavor, but you don't have to quit your day job to make it. Collards also pair well with Double Orange Pork Chops (page 24) and Down-Home Pinto Beans and Ham Hocks (page 127).

SERVES 6

8 strips bacon (about 8 ounces), cut into ½-inch pieces
1 medium Vidalia onion, halved and thinly sliced
2 pounds collards, rinsed and drained, stems removed, leaves cut into ½-inch strips
1 teaspoon salt or to taste
Tabasco or other hot sauce to taste

1. Cook the bacon in a large saucepan over medium-high heat for 5 minutes, or until crisp. Add the onion and cook for 5 minutes more, or until the onion is tender.

2. Add 2 cups of water and simmer for 10 minutes. Add the collards and simmer for about 20 minutes, or until very soft. Season with the salt and Tabasco and serve.

"My secret to healthy food with flavor? Do not be shy about the hot sauce!"
—Bobby

The Deen Family's Pimiento Mac and Cheese

Bobby may just make the best pimiento cheese there is. This version is a combo of Bobby's recipe and the classic Lady & Sons' version. We like to use pimiento cheese everywhere, not just as a dip. Leftovers sometimes find their way onto a burger, and every once in a while, we'll make a batch just for this souped-up mac and cheese, which we often serve with a nice cup of hot tomato soup.

SERVES 6 TO 8

One 8-ounce package cream cheese, at room temperature

4 cups grated cheddar cheese (1 pound)

2 cups grated Monterey Jack cheese (8 ounces)

1 cup mayonnaise

6 tablespoons chopped pimiento

2 teaspoons grated onion

½ teaspoon salt

¼ teaspoon garlic powder

Freshly ground black pepper to taste

1 pound macaroni, cooked and drained

1. Preheat the oven to 400°F.

2. Process the cream cheese in a food processor until smooth. Add 2 cups of the cheddar cheese, the Monterey Jack cheese, the mayonnaise, pimiento, onion, salt, garlic powder, and pepper and pulse to combine.

3. Transfer the pimiento cheese to a large bowl and stir in the macaroni. Spread the mixture into a 9 x 13-inch baking dish and top with the remaining 2 cups cheddar cheese. Bake for 20 to 25 minutes, or until the casserole is golden and bubbly.

Almost Aunt Peggy's Roasted Eggplant and Mozzarella Bake

Our Aunt Peggy does a zucchini bake for every get-together, and it is so good that we decided to try cooking eggplant the same way. Since we don't fry it, this is a healthier, easier take on your standard eggplant Parmesan, and, served over spaghetti with a crisp romaine and tomato salad, it makes a delicious vegetarian meal. (Of course, you can always add grilled chicken breast, if you prefer.)

SERVES 4

1½ pounds eggplant, cut into 1-inch cubes

2½ teaspoons olive oil

Salt and freshly ground black pepper to taste

1 cup prepared tomato sauce

1½ tablespoons chopped fresh basil

1½ cups shredded mozzarella (6 ounces)

1 cup grated Parmesan cheese (4 ounces)

1 cup ricotta cheese (4 ounces)

1. Preheat the oven to 500°F.

2. Toss the eggplant with the olive oil and season with salt and pepper. Place on a baking sheet and roast, tossing occasionally, for 20 minutes, or until golden.

3. Reduce the oven temperature to 425°F. Transfer the eggplant to a 1½-quart baking dish. Add the tomato sauce and basil and toss to coat the eggplant. Layer the mozzarella, Parmesan, and ricotta on top. Bake for 20 to 25 minutes, or until golden.

Crisp Romaine and Tomato Salad

When Jamie craves salad (believe it or not, he does!), this is what he's after: something you can chow down on. Hearty, crunchy romaine is perfect for that. We also love it with Mama's Tasty Baked Beans and Sausage Soup (page 126) and Sautéed Ravioli with Cheese and Bread Crumbs (page 166).

SERVES 4

3 tablespoons olive oil
1½ tablespoons red wine vinegar
1 garlic clove, minced
Pinch of dried oregano
Salt and freshly ground black pepper to taste
6 cups chopped romaine lettuce hearts (about 2 hearts)
1 green bell pepper, seeded and diced
1 cup grape or cherry tomatoes, halved

1. To make the dressing: In a small bowl, whisk together the olive oil, vinegar, garlic, oregano, salt, and pepper.

2. In a large bowl, combine the lettuce, bell pepper, and tomatoes. Add the dressing and toss to combine.

Mama's Yankee White Bean Pies

Mama is friends with a couple from Indiana named the Moyers, who we like to refer to as Yankees. They taught her how to turn a handful of affordable, simple ingredients into these fried-patty sandwiches that will rock your world.

SERVES 6

Two 15-ounce cans cannellini beans, rinsed and drained

1¾ cups crushed Ritz crackers (about 35 crackers)

1 large egg, lightly beaten

1 teaspoon dried thyme

1 teaspoon salt

¾ teaspoon freshly ground black pepper

Olive oil, for frying

1 Vidalia onion, thinly sliced, for serving

Mayonnaise, for serving

12 slices white bread

1. Place the beans in a large bowl. Mash with a fork or potato masher until the beans are almost smooth, but still a little chunky. Add ¾ cup of the cracker crumbs, the egg, thyme, salt, and pepper and mix well. Use your hands to form the mixture into 6 equal-size patties.

2. Place the remaining 1 cup cracker crumbs in a wide shallow bowl. Dip each patty in the cracker crumbs, turning to coat evenly.

3. Heat ⅛ inch olive oil in a large skillet over medium heat until hot, but not smoking. Fry the patties, turning once, until golden, about 3 minutes per side. Drain the patties on a paper-towel-lined plate.

4. Sandwich each patty, along with sliced onion and a dollop of mayonnaise, between 2 slices of bread and serve.

Lemony Coleslaw with Raisins

Prepared shredded coleslaw mix is one of our favorite items in the produce aisle because it's so easy to toss in a bowl—all the work's already done. You can bring this slaw to a potluck supper and get raves, and it takes less than ten minutes to put together. It's no surprise that this is also terrific with Sweet and Spicy Pork (page 128), and kids will love it with Mini Macaroni Pies (page 168).

SERVES 6

One 16-ounce bag coleslaw mix
½ cup plus 2 tablespoons mayonnaise
½ cup golden raisins
½ cup thinly sliced scallions (white and light green parts)
Finely grated zest of 1 lemon
1 teaspoon freshly squeezed lemon juice

½ teaspoon salt
¾ teaspoon freshly ground black pepper

In a large bowl, combine the coleslaw mix, mayonnaise, raisins, scallions, lemon zest, lemon juice, salt, and pepper. Toss well before serving.

crockpot cooking

We're so fortunate that our mama never stopped using her old crockpot. I remember that thing bubbling on the counter, smelling like dinner, even though we were just sitting down for breakfast. Everything that came out of Mama's slow cooker was so tender and savory, whether it was her chicken and dumplings or her pot roast. Those old pots were a staple in Southern kitchens fifty years ago. Now, slow cookers have made a big comeback. You can buy them in any housewares store. Using them takes the pressure off a busy day when you can set up your ingredients early so you don't have to think about dinner until you're sitting down at the table.

One of the great beauties of slow cooking is that the most humble foods come out the best. We never use fancy ingredients; we just throw in some affordable meat and sturdy veggies. By the time this easy combo is done you're eating a four-star meal. The flavors are all sealed in, so you can get the most intense stews this way, without even being in the kitchen.

Anything that gets better as it simmers is great in the crockpot, from our **All-Day Beef Chili** (page 122) to **Bobby's Turkey Vegetable Goulash** (page 132). And when you're feeding a busy household where everyone needs to eat at a different time, that keep-warm function is key.

Recipes that cook a long time almost always last a long time, too. We never met a crockpot dish that didn't taste even better reheated the next day. The faster things get, the more we rely on slow cookers to maintain our standards for homey, comforting stews, braises, sauces, soups, and chilies. Sure, baked beans from a can are darn tasty. But **Mama's Tasty Baked Beans and Sausage Soup** (page 126)? It'll take you ten minutes, and it just might make your week.

All-Day Beef Chili

Serve this hearty chili over rice for a simple meal, or do it up Deen style over a bowl of Fritos corn chips with cheese, fresh onions, and sour cream. It sure tastes good with Moist-and-Easy Corn Bread (page 45).

SERVES 6 TO 8

1 tablespoon olive oil

1½ pounds ground beef

2½ teaspoons The Lady's House Seasoning (page 7)

5 tablespoons chili powder

Four 15-ounce cans kidney beans, rinsed and drained

Three 14½-ounce cans diced tomatoes, drained

1 medium onion, chopped

1 garlic clove, finely chopped

Sour cream, for serving

Grated cheddar cheese, for serving

1. Heat the olive oil in a large skillet over medium-high heat. Add the beef and brown for 5 to 7 minutes, or until the meat is no longer pink. Pour off the drippings and add 1½ teaspoons of the house seasoning and 2 tablespoons of the chili powder.

2. Transfer the beef mixture to the crockpot. Stir in the kidney beans, tomatoes, onion, garlic, the remaining 1 teaspoon house seasoning, and the remaining 3 tablespoons chili powder.

3. Cover and cook on high for 4 hours or on low for 8 hours. Serve hot with a dollop of sour cream and a generous sprinkling of grated cheddar cheese.

"The only thing better than a one-pot supper is a one-pot supper plus leftovers!"
—Bobby

Homey Pot Roast with Root Veggies

PHOTOGRAPH ON PAGE 118

The crockpot might just have been invented to turn out the most tender pot roast you've ever had. Slow cooking makes the meat and veggies here so delicious that you might want to keep the recipe on hand for when company is coming for dinner. We think it's so special that we serve a version of this at The Lady & Sons. And if you make it in advance, this pot roast just keeps getting better. We eat this with Buttery Stone-Ground Grits (page 25) when we get together for a family dinner.

SERVES 4 TO 6

One 5-pound pot roast, rinsed and patted dry

Salt and freshly ground black pepper to taste

2 medium parsnips, peeled and cut into 1½-inch chunks

2 large russet potatoes, peeled and cut into 1½-inch chunks

1 medium onion, peeled and cut into 1½-inch chunks

One 10¾-ounce can cream of potato soup

1 bay leaf

1. Season the roast generously with salt and pepper. Place the parsnips, potatoes, and onion in the bottom of the crockpot. Add the soup and 1 cup of water and stir well to combine. Add the bay leaf. Place the roast on top of the vegetables.

2. Cover and cook on high, turning the meat occasionally, for 8 hours, or until the meat is very tender and shreds easily with a fork. Remove and discard the bay leaf. Serve the roast along with the vegetables.

a bit more, y'all

If you have the time, you can make a delicious sauce by skimming and discarding the fat from the pan juices and puréeing the skimmed juices with the vegetables. Or just serve as is.

Polish Crockpot Stew with Kielbasa and Cabbage

We got this recipe from our good buddy (and Bobby's neighbor) Michael Peay. He remembers his mom always used to make more than he and his brothers ever could eat because their house was so popular with their friends, especially around dinnertime. This stew, full of good porky sausage and plenty of tender cabbage, was his favorite childhood meal.

SERVES 4 TO 6

1 tablespoon olive oil

One 1-pound package kielbasa, sliced into ½-inch-thick rounds

1 medium onion, halved and thinly sliced

1¾ pounds white potatoes, peeled and cubed

1 small cabbage, quartered, cored, and sliced into ribbons

1 tablespoon salt

1 teaspoon freshly ground black pepper

1. Heat the olive oil in a large skillet over medium-high heat. Brown the kielbasa for about 5 minutes. Using a slotted spoon, transfer the meat to the crockpot.

2. Reduce the heat in the skillet to medium and add the onion. Cook, stirring, for 3 to 5 minutes, or until softened. Add ½ cup of water and continue cooking, scraping up the brown bits, for 1 minute more. Add the onion with the liquid to the crockpot. Stir the potatoes, cabbage, salt, and pepper into the crockpot.

3. Cover and cook on high for 1½ hours or on low for 3 hours. Serve hot.

Mama's Tasty Baked Beans and Sausage Soup

One of Bobby's favorite soups on the menu at The Lady & Sons is Confederate bean soup, a rich mix of baked beans, sausage, and cream. We skip the cream here to make a lighter version with just as much flavor as the original. It's a hearty meal in a bowl and a dream come true for anyone who loves franks and beans.

SERVES 4 TO 6

1 tablespoon olive oil

1 medium onion, finely chopped

2 large carrots, peeled and diced

Four 16-ounce cans baked beans

1 pound cooked bratwurst, cut into ¼-inch-thick rounds

1 cup beef or chicken broth

¼ teaspoon salt

¼ cup sliced scallions (white and light green parts), for garnish

1. Heat the olive oil in a large skillet over medium-high heat. Add the onion and cook for 3 to 5 minutes, or until softened.

2. Combine the onion, carrots, beans, bratwurst, beef broth, and salt in the crockpot.

3. Cover and cook on high for 4 hours or low for 8 hours, or until the carrots are tender. Garnish with the scallions and serve hot.

Down-Home Pinto Beans and Ham Hocks

Mama's main squeeze Michael Groover's famous pinto beans inspired this simple, savory recipe. We use a few dashes of Worcestershire sauce to create a real rich broth around the soft, silky beans.

SERVES 4

Four 15-ounce cans pinto beans, rinsed and drained

3 garlic cloves, finely diced

2 celery ribs, finely diced

1 smoked ham hock

1 cup chicken broth

1 large onion, finely diced

1 large carrot, peeled and finely diced

1 teaspoon tomato paste

1 teaspoon salt

1 teaspoon freshly ground black pepper

¾ teaspoon Worcestershire sauce

1. Combine the beans, garlic, celery, ham hock, chicken broth, onion, carrot, tomato paste, salt, pepper, and Worcestershire sauce in the crockpot.

2. Cover and cook on low for 6 hours, then check to make sure the beans are tender. If it's too thin for your taste, uncover and continue to cook for 2 hours more. If not, uncover and cook for 1 hour more, or until thickened.

3. Transfer the ham hock to a cutting board. Remove all the meat from the bone. Chop the meat into pieces and return it to the crockpot, stirring to combine. Serve hot.

"I taught my boys not to look down on an economical cut of meat. That's a cut that just gets better and better the longer it cooks."
—Paula

Sweet and Spicy Pork

We owe enormous thanks to our slow cooker for making it possible to turn our absolute favorite weekend treat, barbecued pork, into a four-ingredient recipe we can throw together for a weeknight. We love to make sandwiches with the soft, flavorful shredded pork on hamburger buns, and serve them with some Lemony Coleslaw with Raisins (page 116), on top or alongside.

SERVES 4

One 3- to 4-pound bone-in Boston pork butt

One 1-ounce envelope Lipton onion soup and dip mix

1 medium onion, quartered

One 12-ounce bottle barbecue sauce or 1½ cups Easy BBQ Sauce (page 91)

1. Score the pork butt in several areas, making cuts 1 inch deep. Rub the soup mix into the meat.

2. Scatter the quartered onion in the bottom of the crockpot and place the meat on top.

3. Cover and cook on high for 4 hours or low for 8 hours.

4. Carefully transfer the meat to a plate and allow it to cool slightly. Strain the liquid remaining in the crockpot through a colander or sieve. Save the meat pieces and onion bits, and discard the liquid and any excess fat. When the pork butt has cooled, remove any excess fat and discard the bone. Using a fork, break up the meat.

5. Place the meat, along with the bits and pieces from the strained liquid, back in the crockpot. Pour the barbecue sauce over the meat and stir to coat well. Heat on the warm setting until ready to serve.

Braised Chicken with Peppers and Mushrooms

Cooking chicken with mushrooms gives you such a nice intense and meaty-tasting broth. Along with meltingly soft bell peppers and onions, this throw-it-all-in-the-pot stew has wonderful Italian flavor. We love it over buttered noodles.

SERVES 4

3 tablespoons olive oil

2½ pounds boneless skinless chicken thighs

One 4-ounce can sliced mushrooms, drained

1 teaspoon dried oregano

Pinch of crushed red pepper flakes

One 14½-ounce can whole peeled tomatoes, drained

1 tablespoon freshly squeezed lemon juice

1 teaspoon salt

4 garlic cloves, finely chopped

2 onions, chopped

2 green bell peppers, seeded and cut into 1-inch chunks

1 red bell pepper, seeded and cut into 1-inch chunks

2 tablespoons chopped fresh basil, for garnish

1. Heat the olive oil in a large skillet over medium-high heat. Add the chicken and brown, turning occasionally, for 7 to 10 minutes. Stir in the mushrooms, oregano, and red pepper flakes and cook for 30 seconds. Stir in the tomatoes and break them up lightly with a fork. Add the lemon juice and salt and simmer for 2 minutes.

2. In a bowl, combine the garlic, onions, and bell peppers. Place half of the mixture in the bottom of the crockpot. Cover with half the chicken and sauce, then layer on the remaining bell pepper mixture and top with the remaining chicken and sauce.

3. Cover and cook on high for 3 hours or low for 4 hours. Garnish with the basil and serve hot.

a bit more, y'all

These leftovers make the best Italian-style hero sandwiches ever!

Quick -'n'- Easy Chicken 'n' Dumplings

Mama's chicken and dumplings are *sooo* good. She simmers her chicken for ages until she has the richest stock—that's how we do it at The Lady & Sons. All that effort certainly pays off, but we just never have time to cook like that. That's where the slow cooker comes in. Along with easy-to-make drop dumplings (Mama would roll hers out), you'll get that hearty chicken flavor and the light, fluffy, comforting dumplings without having to stay by the stove all day.

SERVES 4 TO 6

CHICKEN

One 3½-pound chicken, cut into 8 pieces

2 carrots, peeled and diced

2 celery ribs with leaves, chopped

4 fresh parsley sprigs

2 garlic cloves, minced

1 medium onion, chopped

2½ teaspoons salt

¼ teaspoon freshly ground black pepper

1 bay leaf

DUMPLINGS

1¾ cups Bisquick baking mix

½ cup plus 2 tablespoons milk

2 tablespoons chopped fresh parsley or 2 teaspoons dried parsley

Sour cream, for serving

1. To make the chicken: Place the chicken in the crockpot. Add water to cover, about 2 cups. Add the carrots, celery, parsley sprigs, garlic, onion, salt, pepper, and bay leaf. Cook, covered, on high for 3 hours or low for 7 hours, or until the meat begins to fall from the bone.

2. To make the dumplings: In a large bowl, combine the Bisquick and milk. Stir in the parsley. Drop the batter by tablespoons into the liquid in the crockpot—the dumplings should be just submerged.

3. Cover and cook the chicken and dumplings on high for 40 to 45 minutes, or until the dumplings are tender. Using a slotted spoon, transfer the dumplings to a bowl. Remove and discard the bay leaf. Transfer the chicken and vegetables to another bowl. Once the chicken is cool enough to handle, remove the skin and shred the chicken from the bone (it will be very tender and will shred easily). Discard the skin and bones. If the chicken and dumplings have gotten cold, reheat briefly in a microwave or on the stove top. Serve the chicken and vegetables along with the dumplings and top with a generous dollop of sour cream.

Bobby's Turkey Vegetable Goulash

Bobby loves his goulash. It's still the dish he begs Mama to make for him, even though he can have this easier, leaner version ready for himself when he gets home whenever he likes. Mama often serves her goulash the next day to let the flavors marry; cooking it in a crockpot in a single day achieves the same delicious effect.

SERVES 4 TO 6

2 tablespoons olive oil

2 pounds ground turkey

Two 14½-ounce cans diced tomatoes, drained

One 14½-ounce can tomato sauce

2 garlic cloves, minced

1 large onion, chopped

1 cup frozen corn kernels, thawed

2 tablespoons soy sauce

1½ teaspoons dried basil

1½ teaspoons dried oregano

¾ teaspoon garlic powder

¾ teaspoon salt

¾ teaspoon freshly ground black pepper

4½ cups cooked macaroni (8 ounces uncooked), for serving

Sour cream, for serving

1. Heat the olive oil in a large skillet over medium-high heat. Cook the turkey, breaking it up with a fork, until browned, about 10 minutes.

2. Transfer the meat to a crockpot and add the diced tomatoes, tomato sauce, garlic, onion, corn, soy sauce, basil, oregano, garlic powder, salt, and pepper.

3. Cover and cook on high for 2 hours or low for 4 hours, or until the goulash has thickened and completely cooked through. Serve the goulash over the macaroni and top with a generous dollop of sour cream.

main-course salads

ASIAN-STYLE BEEF AND NOODLE SALAD WITH
CUCUMBERS 138

HEARTY THREE-BEAN-AND-HAM SALAD 139

SAUSAGE AND POTATO SALAD WITH TOMATOES
AND GREENS 140

CLASSIC CHOPPED SALAD 142

PASTA SALAD WITH GRILLED CHICKEN AND
VEGGIES 143

JAMIE'S NUTTY ORANGE CHICKEN SALAD 145

MEDITERRANEAN CHICKEN AND ORZO SALAD
WITH SUN-DRIED TOMATOES AND PINE NUTS 146

CHICKEN AND RICE SALAD WITH
GUACAMOLE 147

TORTELLINI TRICOLORE SALAD 148

SPICY HONEY CHICKEN SALAD OVER
SPINACH 150

There's nothing boring about a salad.

Sure, it can get dull if you're eating the same little side salad with a slice of cucumber on iceberg lettuce every day, but think of a salad as a place to combine in one bowl all the things you love to eat. If you're like Jamie, salad might consist of nuts, goat cheese, and roasted beets, whereas Brooke always buys feta cheese, pine nuts, and dried cranberries to dress up her greens. And Bobby, the biggest salad eater in the family by far, keeps it interesting by mixing up the leaves—romaine hearts one day, spinach the next, store-bought prewashed lettuce mixes from time to time. Sometimes he puts all of these into his **Classic Chopped Salad** (page 142) of the week. You can make a completely different salad for every meal.

A great salad is that much greater with some protein on top, whether you're talking beans, meat, cheese, or nuts. It's also a convenient place for leftover vegetables, pasta, and rice. For Bobby, "being good" at a restaurant means ordering salad and fish (of course, a side of French fries usually sweetens the deal—we're still in the process of developing our dream recipe for French fry salad!). At home, the fish—or chicken, sliced steak, even sausage—goes right in the salad, and that's dinner.

We keep bottled dressings on hand, but for a main-course salad, it's easy to customize a homemade dressing that really brings your ingredients together. We're big on honey mustard, especially when it's got some kick to it, and we've been doing some kind of guacamole dressing for our rice salads since the days when Mama had her first cooking business, The Bag Lady. And then there's the original Southern salad dressing: mayonnaise. We cut the mayo with vinegar or lemon juice and season it well to create the creamiest and most satisfying of dressings.

The most important thing when you're making salad for dinner is that it's filling and hearty. As we Deens believe, you better not mess with dinner. So get out your biggest salad bowl and start tossing!

Asian-Style Beef and Noodle Salad with Cucumbers

Jamie is always in search of good Asian food, which is one of his favorites. We must have had this salad somewhere along the way, because it found its way into Jamie's kitchen recently. With lime, soy sauce, cucumbers, peanuts, and rice noodles (which you can find in the Asian foods aisle of most supermarkets), it's a whole new set of tastes that will no doubt appeal to anyone looking for something new to try. It's also a perfect place to park your leftover steak.

SERVES 4

8 ounces thin rice noodles

¼ cup soy sauce

¼ cup canola or vegetable oil

2 tablespoons rice wine vinegar

2 tablespoons Asian fish sauce

Freshly squeezed juice of 2 limes

1 tablespoon Tabasco or other hot sauce

2 teaspoons honey

2 garlic cloves, minced

3 cups chopped romaine lettuce hearts (about 1 heart)

1 cucumber, peeled and diced

1 red bell pepper, seeded and diced

½ cup chopped fresh cilantro

½ cup chopped roasted salted peanuts

¾ pound cooked steak, sliced into 1- to 1½-inch strips

1. Bring a large pot of salted water to a boil. Cook the rice noodles according to the package directions. Drain and rinse under cold water. Drain well.

2. To make the dressing: In a small bowl, whisk together the soy sauce, canola oil, vinegar, fish sauce, lime juice, Tabasco, honey, and garlic. Reserve 6 tablespoons of the dressing and toss the noodles with the rest.

3. In a medium bowl, combine the lettuce, cucumber, bell pepper, ¼ cup of the cilantro, and ¼ cup of the peanuts.

4. Divide the salad among 4 plates. Top each plate with a quarter of the noodles and a quarter of the steak slices. Drizzle the reserved dressing over the salads and garnish with the remaining cilantro and the remaining peanuts.

a bit more, y'all

You can find fish sauce in the international aisle of large supermarkets. It adds loads of exotic flavor to any Asian-inspired dish.

Hearty Three-Bean-and-Ham Salad

Growing up in the South, we were surrounded by three-bean salads, which are something of an aquired taste. We ate up Mama's beans and ham hocks, but give us kids a cold bean salad and we'd be out the backdoor. Well, now we've seen the error of our ways—plus canned beans seem to be better these days, less mushy and more flavorful. Here we toss them with spicy cheese and leftover ham for a main-course salad that's delicious served with Moist-and-Easy Corn Bread (page 45).

SERVES 4 TO 6

½ cup olive oil

⅓ cup red wine vinegar

2 teaspoons sugar

Salt and freshly ground black pepper to taste

1 pound thick-cut ham steak (from your supermarket's deli counter), cut into ½-inch pieces

One 15-ounce can kidney beans, rinsed and drained

One 15-ounce can chickpeas, rinsed and drained

One 15-ounce can cut green beans, rinsed and drained

2 scallions (white and light green parts), chopped

4 ounces pepper Jack cheese, cut into ½-inch pieces (optional)

1 head Bibb lettuce

1. To make the dressing: In a small bowl, whisk together the olive oil, vinegar, sugar, salt, and pepper.

2. In a medium bowl, combine the ham, kidney beans, chickpeas, green beans, scallions, and pepper Jack cheese (if using). Add the dressing and gently toss until combined.

3. For each portion, arrange 2 leaves of Bibb lettuce to make a bowl on a plate and fill with the bean salad.

a bit more, y'all

This salad gets better as it sits (up to 4 days, refrigerated), so it's perfect for picnics and potlucks.

Sausage and Potato Salad with Tomatoes and Greens

This full and satisfying meal is Jamie's dream salad—heavy on the sausage and spuds. What's not to love?

SERVES 4

1 pound white or Yukon Gold potatoes, scrubbed

¼ cup olive oil

1 pound andouille sausage, sliced into 1-inch-thick rounds

2 teaspoons Dijon mustard

1 garlic clove, minced

Salt and freshly ground black pepper to taste

1 cup halved cherry tomatoes

⅓ cup seeded and diced green bell pepper

3 tablespoons finely chopped red onion

1 tablespoon red wine vinegar

6 cups (about 4 ounces) crisp greens, romaine, or Boston lettuce, for serving

1. Bring a large pot of salted water to a boil. Cook the potatoes for 20 to 25 minutes, or until tender. Drain well, let cool, and cut into chunks.

2. Heat 1 tablespoon of the olive oil in a skillet over medium-high heat. Add the sausage and cook, stirring occasionally, for 5 to 7 minutes, or until browned. Transfer the sausage to a paper towel–lined plate to drain.

3. To make the dressing: In a small bowl, whisk together the mustard, garlic, salt, and pepper. Whisk in the remaining olive oil.

4. In a large bowl, combine the potatoes, sausage, the dressing, the tomatoes, bell pepper, and onion. Add the vinegar and toss well. Taste and adjust the seasonings, if necessary.

5. Divide the greens among four plates and top with the sausage and potato salad.

Classic Chopped Salad

When we were traveling around the country shooting episodes of our Food Network show, *Road Tasted*, we ate lots of fried, barbecued, and sugary food (Hey, it's a tough job but sombody has to do it). Wherever we were, Bobby would seek out a salad for lunch or dinner to add a little balance to his diet. The night he discovered chopped salad, it was love at first sight. He developed this easy weeknight recipe as soon as we were back home. It's a salad that accommodates almost any ingredient—feel free to add your own personal favorites into the mix.

SERVES 4

6 tablespoons olive oil

3 tablespoons freshly squeezed lemon juice

½ teaspoon salt

¾ teaspoon freshly ground black pepper

6 cups chopped romaine lettuce hearts (about 2 hearts)

3 plum tomatoes, chopped (about 1½ cups)

¼ pound sliced ham, cut into ¼-inch strips

2 small cucumbers, peeled, seeded, and diced (about 1½ cups)

1 cup diced cooked chicken

1 avocado, halved, peeled, pitted, and diced

1 cup grated cheddar cheese (4 ounces)

½ cup chopped pimientos

1. To make the dressing: In a small bowl, whisk together the olive oil, lemon juice, salt, and pepper.

2. In a large bowl, combine the lettuce, tomatoes, ham, cucumbers, chicken, avocado, cheddar cheese, and pimientos. Toss with the dressing until well combined and serve.

Pasta Salad with Grilled Chicken and Veggies

This pasta salad is one of Jamie's "greatest hits" meals. It's perfect for leftover grilled or store-bought rotisserie chicken, and it's got everything we could want Jack to eat in it: pasta, chicken, and veggies. A little ranch dressing makes the salad nice and creamy and helps bring all the ingredients together.

SERVES 4

- 2 boneless skinless chicken breast halves
- 3 tablespoons olive oil
- Salt and freshly ground black pepper to taste
- 1 yellow or green bell pepper, seeded and quartered
- 1 red bell pepper, seeded and quartered
- 4 scallions (white and light green parts)
- 8 ounces (2 cups) rotelle pasta
- ½ cup bottled ranch salad dressing
- ½ cup crumbled bacon bits, for garnish

1. Prepare a medium grill or preheat the broiler. If using the broiler, line a rimmed baking sheet with aluminum foil.

2. Brush the chicken with half of the olive oil and season with salt and pepper. Place the chicken on the grill or, if broiling, place it on the prepared baking sheet. Grill or broil 4 inches from the heat, turning once, until the chicken is lightly browned and the juices run clear when it is pricked with a fork, about 8 minutes per side. Transfer to a platter and set aside.

3. Meanwhile, brush the bell peppers and scallions with the remaining olive oil and season with salt and pepper. Place the vegetables on the grill or, if broiling, transfer to the prepared baking sheet. Grill or broil, turning once or twice, for about 4 minutes per side for the peppers and 2 minutes per side for the scallions. Transfer to a platter and set aside.

4. Bring a large pot of salted water to a boil. Cook the rotelle according to the package directions. Drain well and transfer to a large bowl. Cut the chicken, bell peppers, and scallions into 1-inch pieces and add to the pasta. Toss the mixture with the ranch dressing and garnish with the crumbled bacon.

Jamie's Nutty Orange Chicken Salad

Back in the days of The Bag Lady, when Mama was making bag lunches and we were delivering them, she would always make a chicken salad. For the fall and holiday season she would add walnuts and mandarin oranges to make a colorful, festive lunch with a delicious nutty-sweet appeal. This is Jamie's version. It's a hearty, packed-with-protein meal that looks as good as it tastes.

SERVES 4 TO 6

2 cups diced cooked chicken

⅔ cup mayonnaise

2 hard-cooked large eggs, peeled and chopped

½ cup chopped walnuts, toasted

1 celery rib, diced

¼ cup sliced scallions (white and light green parts)

2 teaspoons freshly squeezed lemon juice

1 teaspoon salt

½ teaspoon freshly ground black pepper

4 cups (about 3 ounces) crisp greens, like romaine or Boston lettuce, for serving

One 15-ounce can mandarin oranges, drained, for garnish

1. In a large bowl, combine the chicken, mayonnaise, eggs, walnuts, celery, scallions, lemon juice, salt, and pepper and mix well.

2. Divide the greens equally among four to six plates. Serve the chicken over the greens and garnish with the orange segments.

a bit more, y'all

Mama likes to put halved seedless purple grapes in her salad—you can add them here for a little more fruit and a nice color contrast.

Mediterranean Chicken and Orzo Salad with Sun-Dried Tomatoes and Pine Nuts

PHOTOGRAPH ON PAGE 134

Orzo, a type of pasta shaped like flat grains of rice, is perfect for use in salads because it holds its shape and texture so beautifully. For this heart-healthy meal in a bowl, Jamie was inspired to use Italian flavors like fresh basil, sun-dried tomatoes, and olives, plus Brooke's all-time favorite salad ingredient, pine nuts.

SERVES 4 TO 6

8 ounces (1¼ cups) orzo

1 cup diced cooked chicken

½ cup chopped oil-packed sun-dried tomatoes, drained

½ cup chopped fresh basil

⅓ cup chopped pitted kalamata olives

¼ cup toasted pine nuts

2 tablespoons olive oil

1½ teaspoons freshly squeezed lemon juice

1 garlic clove, finely chopped

¾ teaspoon salt

½ teaspoon freshly ground black pepper

4 cups (about 3 ounces) crisp greens, like romaine or Boston lettuce, for serving

1. Bring a large pot of salted water to a boil. Cook the orzo according to the package directions. Drain well.

2. In a large bowl, combine the orzo with the chicken, sun-dried tomatoes, basil, olives, and pine nuts.

3. To make the dressing: In a small bowl, whisk together the olive oil, lemon juice, garlic, salt, and pepper. Pour the dressing over the salad and toss to combine.

4. Divide the greens equally among four to six plates and serve the chicken and orzo salad on top.

Chicken and Rice Salad with Guacamole

Just about everything Mama makes involves sour cream or mayonnaise. Well, guacamole, with its rich, creamy taste, is like the Mexican version, and it goes great with a chicken and rice salad. This is another Bag Lady cult favorite. People still talk about it—the combination is a real keeper.

SERVES 4 TO 6

3 cups cooked white rice

3 cups diced cooked chicken

2 cups quartered cherry tomatoes

1 cup mayonnaise

¾ cup chopped red onion

¼ cup chopped fresh cilantro

1 jalapeño pepper, seeded and minced

1 teaspoon salt

½ teaspoon freshly ground black pepper

1½ cups prepared guacamole, preferably fresh from your supermarket's refrigerator case, for serving

1. In a large bowl, toss together the rice, chicken, cherry tomatoes, mayonnaise, red onion, cilantro, jalapeño, salt, and pepper.

2. Divide the chicken and rice salad equally among four to six plates and top each serving with a generous dollop of the guacamole.

"I love eating a salad for dinner, but it better be a salad with a capital S, as in Serious!" —Bobby

Tortellini Tricolore Salad

This Italian-inspired salad uses fresh cheese tortellini as its base. (You can find fresh tortellini in the refrigerated section of your local supermarket.) It's a fun variation on the usual pasta salad suspects. Plus, it's superconvenient because you can fix it up to a day ahead and serve it straight from the fridge. We love the way tortellini and mozzarella taste when they've been marinating in Italian seasonings and how nice the colors of the broccoli, tomatoes, and olives look when they are served together. That's why we call this salad *tricolore* (Italian for "three colors")!

SERVES 4 TO 6

½ pound fresh cheese tortellini

¾ pound broccoli, cut into bite-size florets

¾ cup mayonnaise

One ½-ounce packet Italian salad dressing mix

1 teaspoon red wine vinegar, plus additional to taste

2 cups shredded mozzarella (8 ounces)

1 cup diced cooked chicken

1 cup halved cherry tomatoes

¼ cup chopped pitted kalamata olives

1. Bring a large pot of salted water to a boil. Cook the tortellini according to the package directions. Drain well and let cool.

2. Bring a saucepan of water to a boil. Add the broccoli florets and cook for about 2 minutes, until tender but still slightly crisp. Drain and plunge into ice water to stop the cooking. Let cool. Drain well.

3. To make the dressing: In a small bowl, whisk together the mayonnaise, Italian salad dressing mix, and vinegar.

4. In a large bowl, combine the tortellini, broccoli, mozzarella, chicken, cherry tomatoes, and olives. Fold the dressing into the salad. Taste and add more vinegar, if desired.

Spicy Honey Chicken Salad over Spinach

The sweet and spicy dressing on this simple salad is a real winner (and one of Brooke's favorites). You can buy canned chipotle chiles in the Mexican section of most supermarkets. They add the smokiness we usually get from bacon to this healthy spinach salad.

SERVES 4

¾ cup olive oil

¼ cup apple cider vinegar

1 tablespoon plus 1 teaspoon honey

2 chipotle chiles in adobo sauce, seeded (if desired) and finely chopped

1½ teaspoons salt

4 cups diced cooked chicken

⅔ cup peeled and diced cucumber

3 tablespoons finely chopped red onion

6 cups (about 4 ounces) baby spinach

1. To make the dressing: In a small bowl, whisk together the olive oil, vinegar, honey, chipotles, and salt.

2. In a large bowl, combine the chicken, cucumber, and red onion. Reserve ¼ cup of the dressing and toss the rest into the chicken salad.

3. Divide the spinach equally among four plates and top each with the chicken salad. Drizzle each salad with 1 tablespoon of the reserved dressing.

jack's favorites
(kid food)

YUMMY ORANGE BEEF FINGERS 157

BEANIE-WIENIES 158

CHICKEN NUGGETS WITH HONEY-LEMON
DIPPING SAUCE 159

The Lady & Sons Honey Mustard Sauce 159

PECAN CATFISH FISH STICKS 160

EXTRA-SPECIAL GRILLED CHEESE TOASTS
WITH TOMATO 162

CHEESY QUESADILLAS WITH AVOCADO 163

BABY BUTTERMILK BISCUIT PIZZAS 165

SAUTÉED RAVIOLI WITH CHEESE AND
BREAD CRUMBS 166

BAKED HUSH PUPPIES 167

MINI MACARONI PIES 168

PANFRIED PB&J 170

CHEESY CINNAMON TOAST 171

JACK'S JELL-O AND FRUIT SALAD 173

There are a lot of challenges to having a kid. With Jack, one of the hardest, and also most exciting, challenges has been discovering what he likes to eat and coming up with new ways for him to enjoy wholesome foods. You have to know your kid to know how to get him or her interested in eating well. And by *well,* we mean real food that doesn't come only out of cans and boxes.

Our focus is on making meals Jack-friendly, like slicing beef into kid-size pieces that he can eat with his hands. Of course, we grew up loving PB&J, grilled cheese, and hot dogs, and Jack almost always goes for the foods that are typically thought of as "kid food." But we do try as often as possible to make his meals at home, from scratch, so we know what's in them and we're not teaching him to love only fast food.

As kids get older, they usually like to be involved in cooking, so projects like topping their own **Baby Buttermilk Biscuit Pizzas** (page 165) are perfect for having fun with fresh ingredients. Even little kids like Jack enjoy dips—whether we set out a little cup of ketchup or a sauce for dunking **Chicken Nuggets with Honey-Lemon Dipping Sauce** (page 159). But the only hard-and-fast rule about what kids will like is that what they like constantly changes.

One of the things we've learned is to keep it simple. When you spend thirty or forty minutes shopping and putting something together and your kids won't touch it (or, in Jack's case, when he tries to sneak it to our bulldog, Champ), it can be so frustrating. But even then, you have to remember the times when you hit on something that they really like. When Jack eats all of the food we've made and says, *"Mmmm-mmmm-mmm!"* it's the highlight of our day. There's nothing better than giving your child a good meal that he or she loves.

Yummy Orange Beef Fingers

Finger food is a great way to get kids eating real food. These little strips of beef are juicy and tender, with a crunchy panko bread crumb crust—delicious served with the slightly sweet orange dip. Just add a colorful vegetable (carrot sticks, broccoli spears, cherry tomatoes, or bell peppers), and you've got a great kid's meal.

SERVES 4 TO 6 KIDS

1 pound boneless bottom round steaks, cut crosswise into 1-inch strips

Salt and freshly ground black pepper to taste

½ cup all-purpose flour

3 large eggs, lightly beaten

2 cups panko bread crumbs

Vegetable oil, for frying

½ cup orange marmalade

4 teaspoons rice vinegar or white wine vinegar

½ teaspoon Dijon mustard or to taste

1. Season the beef with salt and pepper. Place the flour, eggs, and panko in separate bowls. Dredge the beef strips first in the flour, shaking off any excess, then dip them into the beaten eggs, and then the panko.

2. Heat ½ inch of vegetable oil in a large skillet over medium-high heat. When a crumb of panko sizzles after being dropped in, the oil is ready. Fry the beef strips, turning once, until brown, about 1 minute per side. Transfer the beef to a paper towel–lined plate to drain. Sprinkle with salt.

3. To make the dipping sauce: In a small microwave-safe bowl, stir together the marmalade, vinegar, and mustard. Microwave on high for 45 seconds, or until bubbly. Serve the beef fingers with the dipping sauce alongside.

Beanie-Wienies

When we were kids, we would go on camping trips and eat beanie-wienies out of the pull-top can and pretend to be cowboys. We thought that was just the best thing in the world to eat. When your kids try these, they will, too. Nowadays it's easy to find healthier versions of traditional hot dogs (nitrate-free or turkey, chicken, or soy dogs) and lower-sodium baked beans in most supermarkets. Try a few different varieties and see which ones your kids like most.

SERVES 6 TO 8 KIDS

Two 16-ounce cans baked beans

1 pound hot dogs, sliced into ¼-inch-thick rounds

3 tablespoons ketchup

1 tablespoon packed light brown sugar

2 teaspoons Dijon mustard

Combine the baked beans, hot dogs, ketchup, brown sugar, and mustard in a medium pot over medium-high heat. Simmer, stirring occasionally, for 5 to 10 minutes. Serve immediately.

"When Jack has seconds, it makes my night." —Jamie

Chicken Nuggets with Honey-Lemon Dipping Sauce

Chicken nuggets are so yummy and fun to eat—what kid doesn't beg for them for dinner? We make our own using white meat chicken coated in cornflakes with a little honey-lemon sauce for dipping—it's a healthier alternative to what you get handed to you through your car window.

SERVES 4 KIDS OR 2 ADULTS

½ cup honey

1½ teaspoons freshly squeezed lemon juice

2 skinless boneless chicken breast halves, cut into 2-inch pieces

1 teaspoon salt, plus additional to taste (optional)

¼ teaspoon freshly ground black pepper

1 large egg, lightly beaten

4 cups crushed cornflakes

Canola oil, for frying

1. To make the dipping sauce: In a small bowl, whisk together the honey and lemon juice.

2. Season the chicken with the 1 teaspoon salt and pepper. Place the egg and cornflakes in separate bowls. Coat each chicken nugget with the egg, letting the excess egg drip back into the bowl. Coat the nuggets with the cornflakes. Set aside on a plate.

3. Heat ½ inch of canola oil to 375°F in a deep skillet. Fry the nuggets, turning once, for 3 to 4 minutes per side, or until golden and cooked through. Transfer the nuggets to a paper towel–lined plate to drain. Season immediately with additional salt (if using) and serve accompanied by the honey-lemon dipping sauce.

a bit more, y'all

You can make extras for the grown-ups to nibble on with drinks, too. Try making **The Lady & Sons Honey Mustard Sauce** for the big kids to dip with. In a small bowl combine ¾ cup mayonnaise, 3 tablespoons honey, 2 tablespoons yellow mustard, 1 tablespoon freshly squeezed lemon juice, 2 tablespoons orange juice, and horseradish to taste. Stir, then cover and chill for 2 to 3 hours before serving.

Pecan Catfish Fish Sticks

The nutty crunch of these fish sticks harkens back to that cafeteria offering in name only. So fun and easy to eat, they're a great way to introduce younger generations to eating fish. We got Jack to eat fish by adding pecans to it. Catfish is a real staple here in the South, but if it's not readily available in your area, try using flounder or cod.

SERVES 2 TO 4

⅔ cup pecans, finely chopped

½ cup Ritz cracker crumbs (about 16 crackers)

1¼ teaspoons salt

½ teaspoon freshly ground black pepper

1 pound catfish, cut into ½-inch fingerlike pieces

½ cup mayonnaise

Lemon wedges, for serving

1. Preheat the oven to 400°F. Lightly grease a baking sheet.

2. In a shallow dish, combine the pecans, crackers, salt, and pepper.

3. Coat each fish stick with the mayonnaise, then coat with the pecan mixture. Arrange the fish sticks on the prepared baking sheet.

4. Bake, turning once, for 12 to 14 minutes, or until the fish is cooked through and the coating is golden brown. Serve with lemon wedges.

Extra-Special Grilled Cheese Toasts with Tomato

We've never met a kid who doesn't love grilled cheese—with extra-gooey cheese, please! We like to slip in some tomato, too, which some kids won't eat otherwise. And let's be honest here: You may as well make yourself one of these while you're at it; otherwise your kid's sandwich doesn't have a chance.

SERVES 4 KIDS OR 2 ADULTS

8 slices white bread

4 tablespoons (½ stick) unsalted butter

Four ¾-ounce wedges Laughing Cow cheese or other spreadable mild cheese

½ cup grated mild cheddar cheese (4 ounces)

¼ teaspoon garlic powder

1 large tomato, thinly sliced

1. Spread one side of each bread slice with the butter. Flip the slices and spread the other side with the spreadable cheese. Divide the cheddar cheese among 4 slices of the bread and sprinkle with garlic powder. Top with the tomato and cover each sandwich buttered side out with 1 of the remaining slices of bread.

2. Heat a large skillet over medium heat. Cook the sandwiches, turning once and pressing down with a spatula to help melt the cheese, until golden brown, 2 to 3 minutes per side. Serve warm.

"I'm always sneaking bites off Jack's plate—man, that kid eats well!"—Bobby

Cheesy Quesadillas with Avocado

Brooke is a huge Mexican food fan. In fact, when Jack was one week old, Brooke had such a mean craving that we took him out to a Mexican spot near us. So it's no surprise that Jack has become a big fan, too. And since quesadillas are pretty much Mexican grilled cheese, we make them just to give him a little variety, and use them as an opportunity to get a little avocado (which is chock-full of vitamins and has more potassium than a banana) into his diet.

SERVES 4 KIDS OR 2 ADULTS

Eight 6-inch flour tortillas

2 cups grated Monterey Jack cheese (8 ounces)

1 avocado, halved, peeled, pitted, and finely diced

1. Sprinkle each of 4 tortillas with ¼ cup of the Monterey Jack cheese. Top each with the avocado, then the remaining cheese. Cover with the 4 remaining tortillas.

2. Heat a skillet over medium-high heat. Add the quesadillas, 1 at a time, and cook for 2 to 3 minutes per side, or until the tortillas are golden and the cheese is melted. Serve warm.

a bit more, y'all

If you've got a salsa fan like we do in Jack, you can offer a little mild salsa for dipping.

Baby Buttermilk Biscuit Pizzas

Rather than making pizza dough from scratch, patting out biscuit dough for mini pizzas is a quick, fun shortcut that older kids, like our eleven-year-old niece Lauren, will enjoy joining in on. And the kids can top their own pizzas, too, if they like, piling on the cheese and pepperoni or, if you've got a strange kid who likes them like Bobby always did, with sliced olives.

SERVES 4 TO 6 KIDS

One 12-ounce can refrigerated buttermilk biscuits

½ cup prepared tomato sauce

½ teaspoon dried oregano

2 cups shredded mozzarella (8 ounces)

4 ounces thinly sliced pepperoni rounds (optional)

¼ cup grated Parmesan cheese (1 ounce)

1. Preheat the oven to 400°F. Lightly grease a baking sheet.

2. Place the biscuits on the prepared baking sheet and use the palm of your hand to flatten the dough to ¼ inch in thickness. Divide the sauce evenly among the biscuits, top with a pinch of the oregano, then layer the mozzarella, pepperoni (if using), and Parmesan cheese.

3. Bake until the biscuits are golden and the cheese is melted, about 15 minutes. Allow the pizzas to cool slightly and serve warm.

a bit more, y'all

Buy the pepperoni presliced in packages (found in your supermarket's deli section) to make assembly even easier.

Sautéed Ravioli with Cheese and Bread Crumbs

So many kids only want to eat mac and cheese right from the box. We decided to come up with an alternative dish for Jack—one where Mom and Dad are in charge of quality control. Jack always cleans his plate, so we have to be quick if we want to sneak a few pieces for ourselves!

SERVES 4 KIDS OR 2 ADULTS

16 ounces fresh cheese ravioli, preferably fresh from your supermarket's refrigerator case

8 tablespoons (1 stick) unsalted butter

½ cup plain unseasoned bread crumbs

1 cup grated Parmesan cheese (4 ounces)

Pinch of salt

1. Bring a large pot of salted water to a boil. Cook the ravioli according to the package directions. Drain well.

2. Melt the butter in a large skillet over medium-high heat. When the butter foam has mostly subsided, add the bread crumbs, ½ cup of the Parmesan cheese, and salt. Toss, using a spatula to scrape the brown bits from the bottom of the pan, for about 2 minutes, or until golden.

3. Add the ravioli to the skillet and cook until the pasta is heated through, about 1 minute. Sprinkle with the remaining ½ cup Parmesan cheese and serve.

Baked Hush Puppies

For those of you who aren't familiar with them, hush puppies are crunchy little cornmeal fritters. We always have them at fish fries, and they're a real hit with kids (and everyone else). This is a healthier version of one of our Granny Paul's specialties. We bake them in mini muffin pans to have on hand for a snack. They travel well, too, so they're a great lunch box option.

SERVES 8 TO 10 KIDS OR 4 TO 6 ADULTS

⅔ cup yellow cornmeal

⅓ cup all-purpose flour

1 teaspoon baking powder

¾ teaspoon salt

⅛ teaspoon freshly ground black pepper

½ cup finely chopped onion

⅓ cup milk

2 large eggs, lightly beaten

2 tablespoons unsalted butter, melted

1. Preheat the oven to 450°F. Lightly grease the cups of a 24-cup mini muffin pan or spray with non-stick cooking spray.

2. In a medium bowl, combine the cornmeal, flour, baking powder, salt, and pepper.

3. In a separate bowl, mix together the onion, milk, eggs, and butter. Fold the egg mixture into the flour mixture until the flour mixture is just moistened.

4. Spoon 1 tablespoon of the batter into each of the prepared mini muffin cups. Bake for 10 minutes, or until the hush puppies are firm to the touch and golden brown around the edges.

Mini Macaroni Pies

When Jack's cousin Baby Lizzie first started picking up food and feeding herself, we started making macaroni and cheese in mini muffin pans for her. Big cousin Jack likes to take a large bite, so for him regular muffin pans fit the bill. You can make these in either one. The crispy Ritz cracker crumbs on the outside form a little crust for these pies, making them perfect to eat with your hands. We're not saying they will be much neater than regular mac and cheese, but these sure are fun and delicious.

SERVES 8 KIDS OR 4 ADULTS

1½ cups crushed Ritz crackers (about 35 crackers)

2½ cups grated cheddar cheese (10 ounces)

4 tablespoons (½ stick) unsalted butter, melted, plus 2 tablespoons cold unsalted butter, cut into pieces

4½ cups cooked elbow macaroni (8 ounces uncooked), drained and kept hot

2 large eggs, beaten

½ cup milk

¼ cup sour cream

¼ teaspoon salt

1. Preheat the oven to 350°F. Lightly grease 8 cups of a 12-cup muffin pan.

2. In a bowl, combine the crackers, 1 cup of the cheddar cheese, and the melted butter. Divide the mixture among the prepared muffin cups and press firmly in the bottom and up the sides of the cups.

3. In a large bowl, mix the macaroni with ½ cup of the cheddar cheese. In a small bowl, combine the eggs, milk, sour cream, cold butter pieces, and salt. Stir the milk mixture into the macaroni.

4. Spoon 2 tablespoons of the macaroni mixture into each cracker crust and top with the remaining cheddar cheese. Bake for about 25 minutes, or until the cheese is browned and slightly crispy. Allow the pies to cool slightly before unmolding and serving warm.

Panfried PB&J

PHOTOGRAPH ON PAGE 152

Unless you're Jamie Deen, you probably need to have a kid around to make yourself one of these melty, divine sandwiches. Add banana instead of jam and you've got yourself Elvis's favorite sandwich.

SERVES 4 KIDS OR 2 ADULTS

2 tablespoons sugar

1½ tablespoons ground cinnamon

4 tablespoons (½ stick) unsalted butter

8 slices white bread

6 tablespoons favorite jam

6 tablespoons creamy peanut butter

1. In a small bowl, combine the sugar and cinnamon.

2. Spread the butter on one side of each bread slice. Flip 4 slices over and spread them with the jam. Flip the remaining slices over and spread them with the peanut butter. Sandwich together the jam slices and the peanut butter slices, keeping the buttered sides of the bread facing out.

3. Heat a large skillet over medium-low heat. Add the sandwiches and sprinkle the cinnamon sugar over the tops. Cook for 2 to 3 minutes, or until the bottoms are golden brown. Flip the sandwiches over and sprinkle the tops with cinnamon sugar. Continue to cook for 2 to 3 minutes, or until the bottoms are golden brown.

4. Remove the sandwiches from the skillet and cut into quarters. Serve, with the crusts on or off, depending on your child's preference.

Cheesy Cinnamon Toast

Mama used to make us cheese toasts and cinnamon toasts for breakfast. (She would leave the oven door open after making them, so we could warm up on chilly mornings.) We started to play with that for Jack, and came up with these tasty cream cheese sandwiches sprinkled with cinnamon sugar. They taste a bit like a cinnamon raisin bagel with cream cheese, but the crunch of the sugar on the outside and the creamy cheese inside make them way more interesting. Plus the cream cheese adds protein, so they're heartier than your average serving of cinnamon toast.

SERVES 4 KIDS OR 2 ADULTS

¼ cup sugar

¼ teaspoon ground cinnamon

4 slices white bread, toasted

¼ cup cream cheese
   (2 ounces)

1. Preheat the broiler. Line a rimmed baking sheet with aluminum foil.

2. In a small bowl, combine the sugar and cinnamon.

3. Spread each slice of toast with 1 tablespoon of the cream cheese and sprinkle with the cinnamon sugar. Transfer the toasts to the prepared baking sheet.

4. Broil, 4 inches from the heat, for 1 to 2 minutes, or until the cinnamon sugar is melted.

Jack's Jell-O and Fruit Salad

Jack could eat fruit all day long, especially berries. He is enamored with different colors and shapes, so to set them off, we love to make him these sweet, jiggly salads. We serve them at playdates with his friends Lex, Brady, and Colin (they're triplets, y'all) and make a game of digging up the fruit in the Jell-O (yup, with their hands—it's messy!).

SERVES 6 TO 8 KIDS

Two 6-ounce packages strawberry Jell-O

½ cup hulled, sliced strawberries

½ cup blueberries

½ cup halved green grapes

½ cup thickly sliced bananas

1. In a large bowl, combine the Jell-O with 2 cups of boiling water. Stir until the powder dissolves completely, about 2 minutes. Stir in 2 cups of cold water. Pour the mixture into a 3-quart Jell-O mold and refrigerate for 30 minutes.

2. Stir in the strawberries, blueberries, grapes, and bananas. Return the mold to the refrigerator and continue to chill until very firm, about 3 hours. Unmold and serve cold in bowls.

no-fuss desserts

We love desserts way too much to give them up, no matter how busy we get. Good thing we're good at finding a way to fix something sweet even when we're short on time and ingredients. Where some people might grab a handful of chocolate chips or a spoonful of peanut butter when they're rummaging around the kitchen after dinner, we're more inclined to really make something we can sit down to together. We figure treats are one of the nicest things to share, and a few nights a week, we like to be able to bring out a sweet surprise after dinner. And no-baking-required desserts like these are so easy to prepare, they're ready to eat in the time it takes for the kids to clear the table.

Sometimes dessert is fruit or we take it a step further by making a blender shake or smoothie, but other nights, we're just improvising with what's in the pantry (cookies, Marshmallow Fluff, and chocolate, for sure!) and the freezer (no Deen freezer is without whipped topping and ice cream). You'll be amazed by the ratio of compliments at the table to time in the kitchen when you combine leftover brownies with frozen fruit and instant pudding for our **Quick Brownie-Raspberry Trifle** (page 183) or blackberry jam and whipped cream for a **Ten-Minute Blackberry Cream Pie** (page 186).

Dessert is a good time to work a little more fruit into your diet, and fruit is a delicious way to lighten up cakes, cookies, or even ice cream. But when it comes to desserts, rather than simply obeying our sweet tooth, we also try to make something that looks great and feels special. That way, we're not tempted to sneak back into the kitchen and start the search all over again! So enjoy, and when you're finished, you can sit back and look at how good a homemade dessert makes everyone feel. That's what really keeps us cookin'.

Double Strawberry Shortcake

Bobby loves biscuits soaked in gravy, and he loves cake soaked in berry juice, so you can bet he's always loved Mama's shortcake. Our version ups the ante with some fluffy pink strawberry whipped cream that is so pretty that you just know it's going to taste like heaven.

SERVES 6 TO 8

1 pint strawberries, washed and hulled

2 tablespoons sugar

1½ cups heavy cream

3 tablespoons strawberry jam, softened

One 9-inch store-bought pound cake loaf

1. In a bowl, gently mix the strawberries and sugar and let sit at room temperature for at least 15 minutes and up to 1 hour.

2. Using an electric mixer, whip the cream just until it thickens. Add the strawberry jam and continue to whip until soft peaks form, 30 seconds to 1 minute more.

3. Slice the pound cake into 1-inch-thick pieces. Place 2 cake slices on each serving plate. Divide the strawberries among the plates, spooning them onto the middle of the pound cake. Top each serving with a generous dollop of the strawberry cream.

"The English call dessert pudding. I call pudding breakfast, lunch, and dinner."
— Jamie

Chocolaty PB&J Ritz Cracker Treats

We heard about peanut butter–topped Ritz cracker treats from a friend in the Midwest. This is our down-South version, tricked out with both jam and chocolate.

MAKES 20 TREATS

20 Ritz crackers

2 tablespoons favorite jam

½ cup creamy peanut butter

**One 12-ounce package milk
chocolate chips**

1. Line a baking sheet with parchment or waxed paper.

2. Arrange the crackers on the prepared baking sheet. Spread about ¼ teaspoon of the jam on top of each cracker. Spread about 1 teaspoon of peanut butter on top of the jam.

3. Place the chocolate chips in a shallow microwave-safe dish. Microwave on medium power for 2 to 4 minutes, stirring every 30 seconds, until completely smooth. Spoon about 1 tablespoon of the hot melted chocolate over each cracker. Using the back of a spoon, gently spread the chocolate over the entire cracker.

4. Transfer the baking sheet to the refrigerator and chill for 30 minutes, or until the chocolate sets.

Chocolate-Dipped Frozen Bananas with Coconut

Bobby's dream is to retire to a beach in the Caribbean and sell frozen chocolate-covered bananas on a stick (see A Bit More, Y'all). He'd be open from noon to one, just long enough to eat lunch and read the paper. The hoped-for sales for each day would be six bananas. Seeing how this dream is not coming true any time soon, he'll just have to settle for these island-inspired delights. We roll them in coconut for that tropical taste, and since they're mostly fruit, they're a pretty healthy dessert or snack. For an extra-special treat, roll them in the crushed candy or cookie topping of your choice.

SERVES 6 TO 8

One 12-ounce package semi-sweet chocolate chips

1 tablespoon vegetable oil

2 cups sweetened coconut flakes

4 large bananas, halved

1. Place the chocolate chips into a shallow microwave-safe dish. Microwave on medium power for 2 to 4 minutes, stirring every 30 seconds. When the chocolate is melted, stir in the vegetable oil.

2. Place the coconut in a separate shallow dish and break up any clumps with your fingers. Spear each banana half with a wooden stick, starting from the wider cut side of the banana and going two-thirds of the way up.

3. Holding on to the stick, dip the banana in the chocolate and turn to coat evenly. Roll the chocolate-covered banana in the dish of coconut and transfer the banana to a plate lined with waxed paper or aluminum foil. Repeat with the rest of the bananas. Place the plate in the freezer for at least 20 minutes and up to eight hours. Serve cold, on the stick.

a bit more, y'all

You can find wooden ice cream sticks for sale at most craft stores and from numerous Internet purveyors, or substitute bamboo grilling skewers, cut in half.

Quick Brownie-Raspberry Trifle

This simple dessert comes together fast, but with layers of pudding, bananas, whipped cream, raspberry jam, and brownies, it's over-the-top fabulous-tasting.

SERVES 4 TO 6

3 cups heavy cream

3 tablespoons instant vanilla pudding mix

1 tablespoon confectioners' sugar

2 teaspoons pure vanilla extract

1 pound brownies, cut into ½-inch chunks (about 4 cups)

¾ cup raspberry jam

3 medium bananas, thinly sliced

1. Using an electric mixer, whip the cream, pudding mix, confectioners' sugar, and vanilla until stiff peaks form.

2. In a large bowl, place 1 cup of the whipped cream mixture. Cover with one-third of the brownies in a single layer. Top with 4 tablespoons of the raspberry jam, then one-third of the sliced bananas. Repeat with two more layers of each ingredient, ending with sliced bananas. Finish off by topping it all with the remaining whipped cream mixture. Chill in the refrigerator for 30 minutes and up to eight hours before serving.

Chocolate-Peanut Butter Malteds

It has been successfully argued that these soda fountain favorites are a good source of protein—after all, they're full of milk and peanut butter. We try to drink them regularly for that reason alone.

SERVES 2

4 scoops chocolate ice cream (about 2 cups)
½ cup milk
½ cup creamy peanut butter
⅓ cup malted milk powder

1. Place the ice cream, milk, peanut butter, and malted milk powder in a blender and pulse to combine.

2. Divide the mixture between two tall glasses and serve with straws.

a bit more, y'all

This one is for all the moms and dads: Make this thicker-than-thick shake and serve it with a straw that's just a little too skinny—and have your camera ready to capture the funny faces!

Cherries Jubilee

Warm, boozy cherries over ice cream is a classic dessert, and it's so easy to do. We like ours over chocolate ice cream (but when Bobby doesn't quite have the energy to make this, you know he's always got Cherry Garcia in the freezer).

SERVES 6 TO 8

Two 16-ounce cans whole cherries in juice, drained and juice reserved

1 tablespoon sugar

1 tablespoon cornstarch

¼ cup kirsch, Cognac, or freshly squeezed orange juice

1 quart chocolate ice cream

1. In a small bowl, whisk together ¼ cup of the reserved cherry juice, the sugar, and cornstarch until the sugar and cornstarch dissolve.

2. Combine the remaining cherry juice and the cornstarch mixture in a large skillet over medium heat. Cook, stirring occasionally, until thickened, about 2 minutes. Stir in the cherries and kirsch and cook until the cherries are warmed through, about 2 minutes more.

3. Place 2 scoops of ice cream in each serving dish. Divide the warm cherry topping among the dishes and serve.

Ten-Minute Blackberry Cream Pie

This is an easy-to-assemble pie that really takes us back to our childhoods. Black-berries grow wild all over Georgia, and coming from a family of great pie bakers, we were always motivated to pick them.

SERVES 6 TO 8

One 10-ounce package fresh or frozen blackberries (thawed if frozen)

3 tablespoons blackberry jam

One 8-ounce tub Cool Whip whipped topping

One 9-inch store-bought graham cracker piecrust

1. Place the blackberries in a bowl and mash with a fork until broken up. Add the jam and mix until combined.

2. Spoon the blackberry mixture into the crust. Top with Cool Whip and serve. `

"If I didn't have a little something sweet at the end of a meal, well, I guess I'd never know the meal had ended."
— Uncle Bubba

Two Brothers' Banana Splits

Guess whose is whose. Yogurt and sorbet with fresh fruit is a luscious and healthful way to get your sundae fix. Or you can go whole hog and pile on the ice cream, peanut butter, fudge, and cookies! As kids growing up, we always got single scoops at the Dairy Queen; we couldn't ask for the banana split—it was the most expensive thing on the menu. It's safe to say we've made up for lost time on that one, though!

SERVES 1

Healthy Guy's Banana Split

1 banana, halved lengthwise
1 scoop favorite sorbet
1 scoop favorite frozen yogurt
Fresh berries, for serving

Place the banana halves in a banana split dish or shallow bowl. Nestle the scoops of sorbet and frozen yogurt between the halves. Serve topped with the berries.

Big Guy's Banana Split

1 banana, halved lengthwise
¼ cup creamy peanut butter
2 scoops favorite ice cream
2 scoops second-favorite ice cream
Whipped cream, for serving
Crumbled cookies, such as Oreos or Nutter Butters, for serving
Chopped honey-roasted peanuts, for serving

Place the banana halves in a banana split dish or shallow bowl. Spread the peanut butter on the cut side of each half. Nestle the ice cream scoops between the halves, alternating the flavors. Serve with a generous dollop of whipped cream, crumbled cookies, and peanuts.

Fluffy Oatmeal Raisin Sandwich Cookies

As a kid, whenever he got the chance, Bobby ate those store-bought oatmeal pies. These are his "grown-up" version.

MAKES 6 SANDWICH COOKIES

Hot fudge sauce

12 large oatmeal raisin cookies

Marshmallow Fluff

Spread a small dollop of fudge sauce on the bottoms of 6 of the cookies. Spread a large dollop of Marshmallow Fluff on the bottoms of the remaining cookies. Sandwich the spread sides of the cookies together and serve.

Brooke's Light and Lovely Peach Parfaits

Brooke is a Georgia girl, so during peach season, she just loves to eat as many peaches as she can. We came up with this pretty, layered dessert for her. Just like Brooke, it's light, lovely, and as Southern as it comes.

SERVES 4

- 4 ripe peaches (about 2 pounds), diced
- 4 teaspoons packed light brown sugar
- ½ teaspoon ground cinnamon
- ½ cup crumbled Sandies pecan shortbreads (about 10 cookies), plus additional for garnish
- Reddi-wip topping

1. In a medium bowl, toss the peaches with the brown sugar and cinnamon.

2. Place a layer of the peaches in the bottom of a parfait glass. Sprinkle the peaches with a large pinch of cookie crumbs and top with Reddi-wip. Repeat with two more layers of each ingredient, ending with Reddi-wip. Garnish with an additional sprinkle of cookie crumbs. Repeat with the remaining parfait glasses. Serve immediately or chill up to 4 hours before serving.

Southern Ambrosia Snowballs

PHOTOGRAPH ON PAGE 174

We always know the holidays are just around the corner when Mama breaks out her ambrosia balls. Our version features marmalade, wafer cookies, and coconut all balled up. Plus, our snowballs are no-bake, so you can fix these festive treats fast and invite the kids to help.

MAKES 24 SNOWBALLS

5 tablespoons light corn syrup

3 tablespoons orange marmalade

2 tablespoons orange liqueur or orange juice concentrate

One 12-ounce box Nilla Wafers, finely crushed

48 mini marshmallows

1¾ cups sweetened coconut flakes

1. In a bowl, combine the corn syrup, orange marmalade, and orange liqueur. Stir in the crushed vanilla wafers until moistened and knead together until well mixed.

2. Use your hands to shape the mixture into 1-inch balls, filling each with 2 mini marshmallows. Roll each ball in the coconut to coat and store in an airtight container for up to 1 week.

a bit more, y'all

If you're serving this dessert right after you prepare it, try sticking half a maraschino cherry in the center of each snowball for an extra surprise.

Quick Chocolate Crunch Banana Pudding

We will not rest until we have consumed every version of banana pudding the South has to offer. Mama's recipe is our gold standard, but it takes more time than we like to spend, so we were determined to come up with a faster take. We are proud to say we've been very successful, even by Mama's standards.

SERVES 6

One 3.4-ounce package instant vanilla or banana pudding mix

2 cups milk

1 teaspoon pure vanilla extract

3 bananas, sliced into ½-inch-thick rounds

1 cup crushed chocolate wafer cookies (about 24 cookies)

Fresh whipped cream or whipped topping

1. Prepare the pudding with the milk according to the package directions. Stir in the vanilla.

2. Arrange the bananas in the bottom of an 8-inch baking dish. Layer ¾ cup of the cookie crumbs over the bananas and spread the pudding over the cookies. Top with whipped cream and garnish with the remaining ¼ cup cookie crumbs.

Index

about the authors

JAMIE and BOBBY DEEN grew up in Georgia—first in Albany and then in Savannah—and, as with many Southerners, cooking and food has always been a big part of their lives. When their mother, Paula Deen, started a sandwich delivery business in 1989, the boys took charge of deliveries. As the business grew into The Lady restaurant, they continued to help. Then, in 1996, the trio opened The Lady & Sons Restaurant to resounding success. They haven't looked back since. They regularly appear on ABC's *Good Morning America* and had their own Food Network show, *Road Tasted*.

MELISSA CLARK has written for *The New York Times, Food & Wine, Travel & Leisure,* and *Real Simple* and has collaborated on twenty-one cookbooks.